Visionary Art

BY THE SAME AUTHOR

VISIONARY HEALING
Psychedelic Medicine and Shamanism
(2022)

Visionary Art

of

Alexander Shester

paintings & commentaries by
Alexander Shester, M.D.

(Expanded Edition)

REGENT PRESS
Berkeley, California
2025

[paperback]
ISBN 13: 978-1-58790-711-1
ISBN 10:1-58790-711-9

[e-book]
ISBN 13: 978-1-58790-712-8
ISBN 10: 1-58790-712-7

Library of Congress Control Number: 2025937287

First Printing - May 1, 2025
Second Expanded Edition - January 1, 2026

Manufactured in the U.S.A.
REGENT PRESS
Berkeley, California
www.regentpress.net

TABLE OF CONTENTS

INTRODUCTION TO VISIONARY ARTWORK

What are visions, and where do they come from? Psychologically, they break through from our unconscious realm, revealing buried truths in symbolic images that are difficult to interpret. They are like dreams, but often more vivid. Perhaps the brain, acting as a receiver, picks up these images and teachings from a universal energetic cosmic field of consciousness, and then resides in the deepest realm of the psyche, the collective unconscious, the transcendental domain, which contains the entire history and evolution of the planet and the cosmos. We then give this vision form and shape, and it becomes conscious as our reality. As a transmitter, the brain can communicate this reality to others. According to quantum physics, human observation can change the outcome of an experience. It is the wisdom of the universe that human consciousness can potentially receive, transmit, and understand how nature and all cultures are interconnected.

After a 34-year hiatus (since 1989), I resumed creating artwork with colored pencils, ink, and acrylics, my preferred media. I participated in numerous guided entheogenic journeys with a shamanic orientation during that time. The visual and wisdom teachings accompanying these adventures into the transpersonal realms motivated me to create visionary art pieces that encapsulate the imagery I witnessed. The first six images are my most recent, completed from 2023-2025, and represent a collage of various ventures to inner space that reinforced my interest in healing and visioning as a practitioner. They reaffirmed my spiritual beliefs and love of the natural world through direct experience and a connection with the unity of the Divine Mind.

The outcomes of all these journeys inspired my creative forces and desire to manifest them in writing, music, and artwork. It became especially important to me after retiring from my career as a psychiatrist, when I no longer had the responsibilities my profession required. Life must always go on until it ends; finding something meaningful to express in one's golden years reinforces the vitality necessary to go onward and inward to find meaning. This is the time in my life when I can experience productivity without the burden of ambition.

Entheogenic Plant Visions

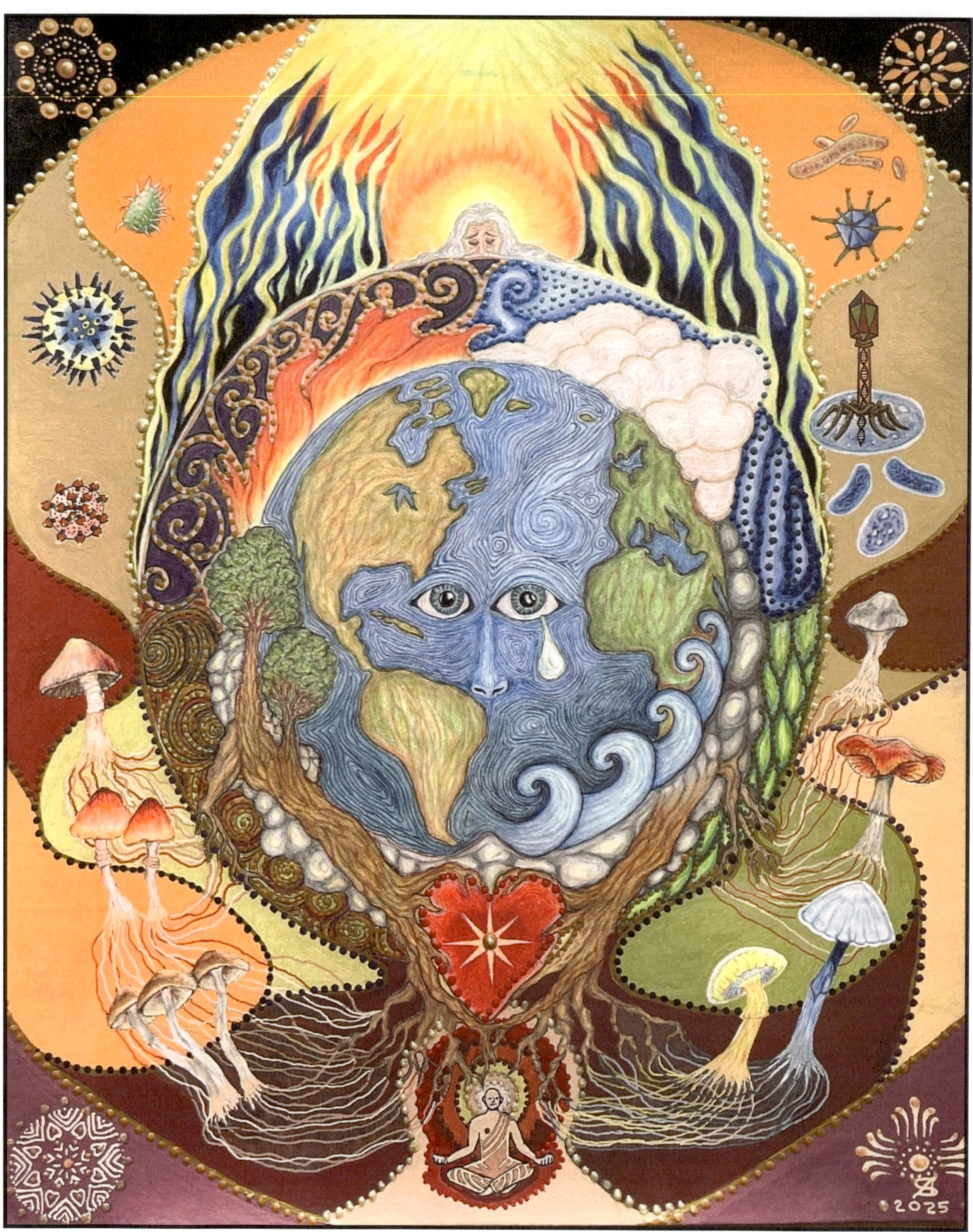

THE BRILLIANT EARTH

I created this painting for the cover of my third book, *The Brilliant Earth: Nature and the Human Psyche.* This book is about humanity's relationship with the natural world, how we participate in the decline of the Earth's health, and how we can change our values to promote the healing of our home, Gaia, the ancient Greek Earth goddess.

The central image portrays Mother Earth weeping over the current state of our planet. Surrounding the Earth are the four elements of Fire, Air, Water, and Earth. The roots of the trees embrace a heart, her gift to humanity, asking us for love, participation, and stewardship. Above is a male godhead figure who also peers down in sadness at what he sees as a degradation of our world. Above him, the sun's life-fire brilliance shines down, its cosmic energy blessing the Earth. Below, a man meditates, mindfully, on the present state of our planet, with the hope that humanity will change the trajectory of its carelessness toward the environment.

On the lower halves of each side, mushrooms are depicted with their mycelial projections connecting to the roots of the trees, communicating information about the local ecosystem. Some scholars view the vast underground mycelial networks as the brain of the Earth, functioning like a network of neurons, sharing information with the plant and animal realms about environmental threats to their health and survival.

On the upper halves of each side are viruses and bacteria that represent their coevolution with animals, plants, and humans. Virus particles appear as spiky and oddly shaped structures (as seen when viewed through an electron microscope) that help them attach to living cells so they can multiply. On the right is seen a virus particle in a shape reminiscent of a lunar lander, injecting DNA or RNA into a cell, thereby imparting new genetic information that enhances adaptation to changing environmental conditions, promotes evolution, or causes cell death, depending on natural selection.

In its entirety, this piece describes the brilliance of the Earth as a form of our planet's intelligence, and perhaps a type of consciousness that promotes homeostasis, self-regulation, symbiosis, reciprocity, adaptability, and cooperation within various planetary ecosystems. Nature can teach us these values. The key is to cultivate humility first.

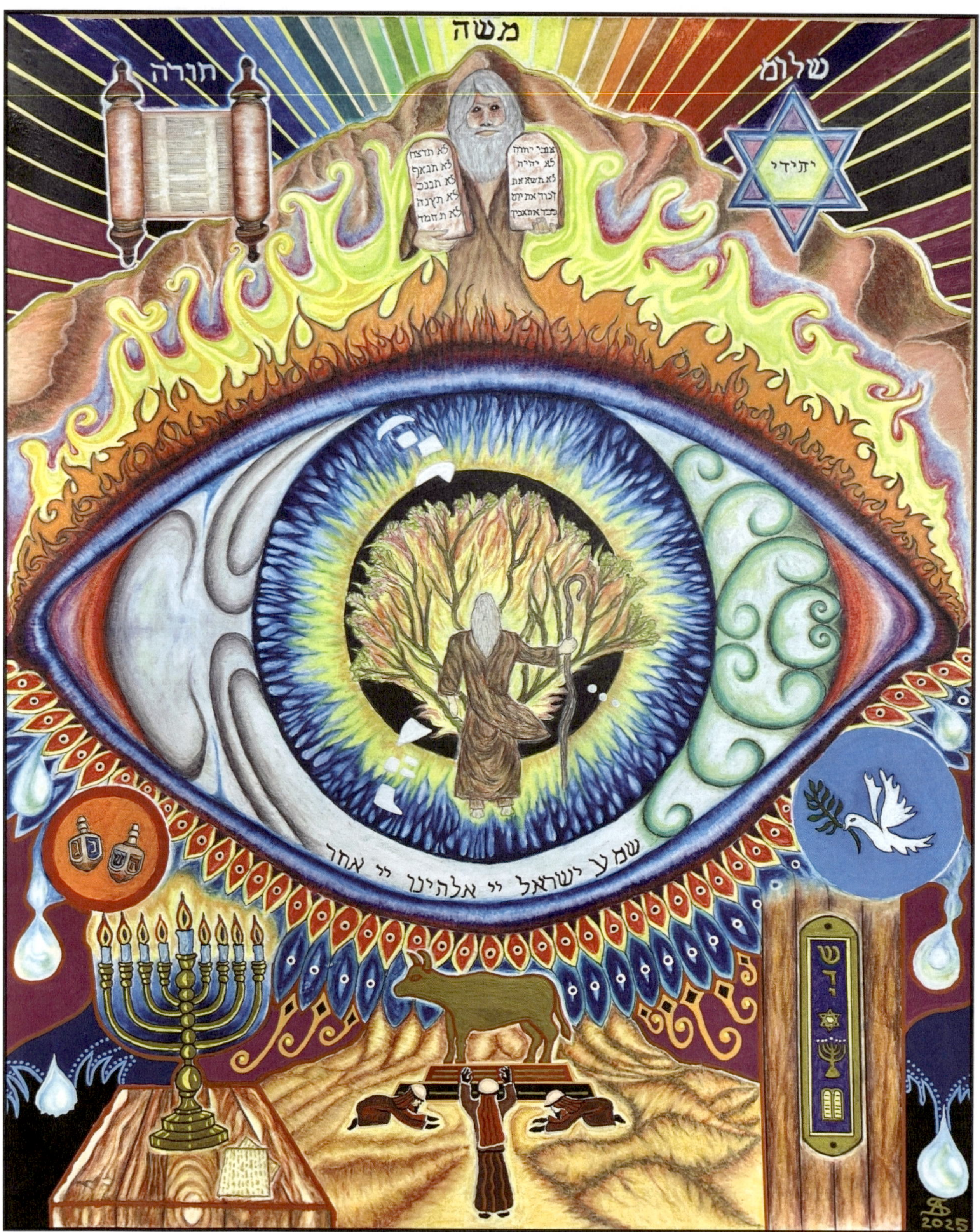

משה
חורה
שלום
יחידי
שמע ישראל יי אלהינו יי אחד

YEHUDI – MOSES AT THE BURNING BUSH BECOMING ENLIGHTENED

I completed this art piece on May 16, 2025, and am entitling it *Yehudi,* which is "Jew" in Hebrew. I wanted to honor my Jewish roots and heritage, although I have become disengaged from the practice of any organized religion. While I identify with the Jewish culture, its rich tradition of ritual, and the spirituality of the Kabbalah, I do not relate to its present dogma.

In the piece, the central image is Moses, reflected in the eye of consciousness, as he witnesses the burning bush on Mount Sinai and is enlightened by God. Perhaps his days of isolation and meditation on the mountain top were similar to the experience of a vision quest, during which he had a visionary encounter and experienced the Divinity face to face. In Exodus 33:20 is stated: "You cannot see my face, for a man cannot see me and live." Spiritually, this implies the death of the ego of the prepared initiate, which occurs before one can merge with the transpersonal realm and receive wisdom. This illumination for Moses culminated in his receiving the Ten Commandments, which he brought to his Jewish brethren in the desert below. Here, he finds them worshipping a false idol, the Golden Calf, representing their identification with materiality and their loss of spiritual identity. Above Moses, the Hebrew letters of his name appear.

Included in the imagery are symbols of Jewish ritual: the Mogan David, the Jewish star, and in its center, the Hebrew script, *Yehudi,* and above, *Shalom.* In the upper left appears the sacred *Torah*, which contains the Pentateuch, the first five books of the Old Testament. *Torah*, in Hebrew, is inscribed above. On the lower inside of the eye is the Hebrew inscription recited by Jews in prayer. "Shema Yisroel Adonai Eloheynu Adonai Ehad – Hear O Israel the Lord our God, the Lord is One."

Other Jewish symbols, including the dreidel, the menorah, the dove of peace, and the mezuzah, are depicted. The Hebrew Shaddai, seen in the mezuzah, is another name for God and implies that he will protect your household. The custom of hanging the mezuzah by a doorway originated during the Passover and identified a Jewish home, chosen to survive the plagues in Egypt. Finally, at the lower edges, tears of both sorrow and joy appear, symbolizing the deep emotions experienced throughout Jewish history.

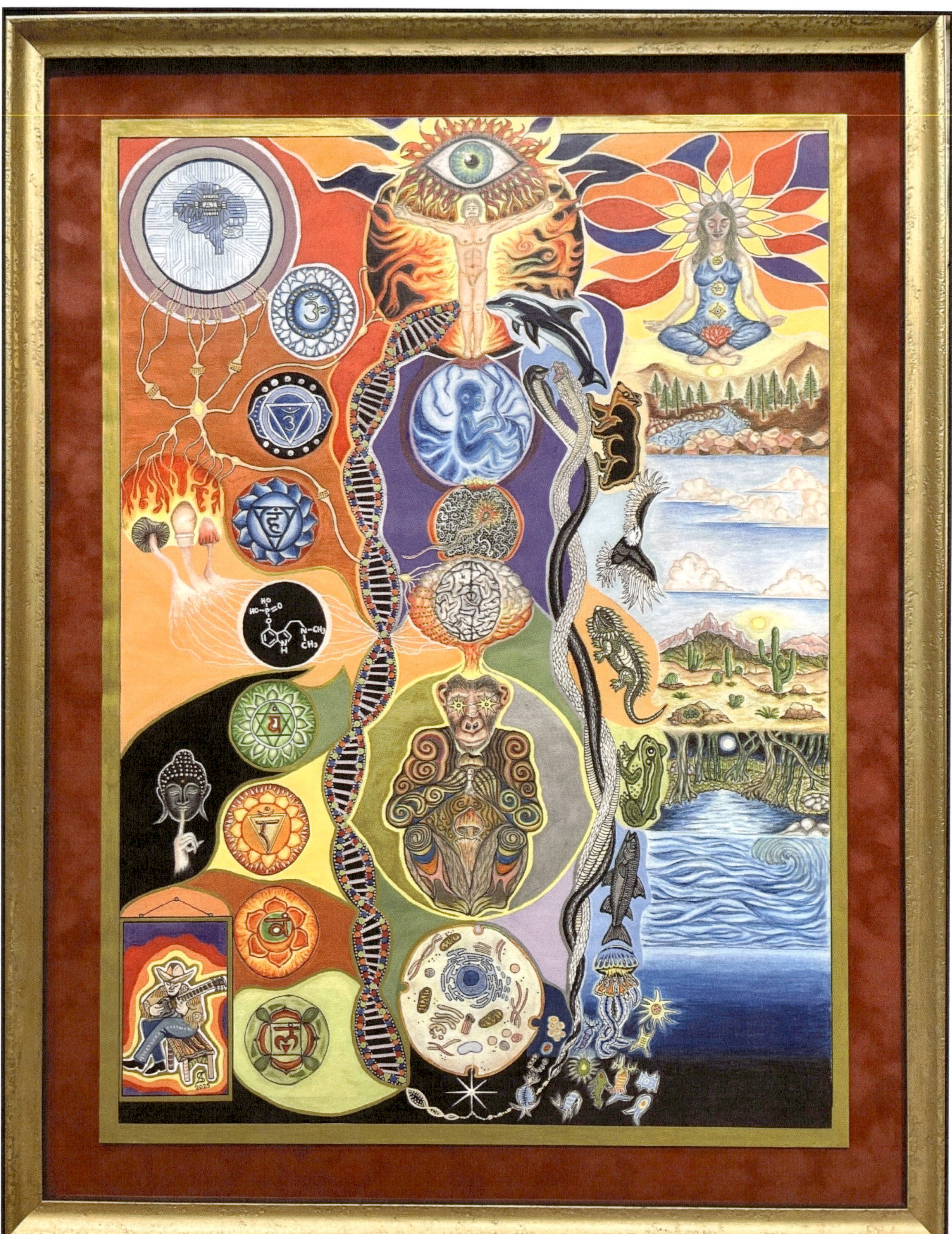

EVOLUTION OF CONSCIOUSNESS

This is the artwork I completed on February 1, 2025, which is based on my shamanic journeys and a meditation called the "Well of Remembrance." The bottom of the vertical totem represents the unseen (in black) of the deep ocean and the universe. A star appears, representing the Big Bang or Big Inflation, out of which the universe becomes known in time and space, eventually creating trillions of galaxies, stars, and planets and finally evolving life on Earth. Pictured is the anatomy of a single cell containing its nucleus with DNA and the mitochondria, which provide energy. The central theme is that of an ape eating a magic mushroom. Its mind explodes with a new consciousness, portrayed by the atomic explosion on top of its head. Inside is a brain symbolizing the mind. If you look carefully in the center of the brain with its grooves (sulci), you will see an abstract image of an embracing couple.

A theory to explain the development of higher awareness, evidenced by the rapid growth of the brain from 500 cc to 1500 cc in a relatively short period of evolutionary time, is known as the Stoned Ape theory; it suggests this brain growth was spawned by mushroom intelligence infiltrating the human brain. Developed by Terrance and Dennis McKenna and still controversial, the theory maintains that when arboreal apes descended from the trees to the ground, they came upon psilocybin mushrooms growing in the dung of some land mammals and used them as food sources, but they also created unexpected visions. This idea corresponds to the opening movie sequence of Stanley Kubrick's *2001: A Space Odyssey*, in which a monolith structure appears. When the apes touch it, a quantum leap in consciousness occurs.

Moving up the totem, one sees the image of a sperm fertilizing an egg, signifying the fertilization process of evolution to the human being. The developing human fetus is seen, and eventually, the higher Man (or Woman) appears in all its glory with arms extended to embrace conscious life, depicted by the all-seeing eye of awareness. The flames represent an abundance of energy. Balancing the male figure, a female in a meditation pose also symbolizes higher consciousness.

Moving outside the central totem to the left, one sees evolution represented by the DNA double helix strand. On the right side are two dark and light serpents, symbolizing the rising feminine Shakti Kundalini energy awakening from the base Chakra as it moves upward to unite with higher masculine Shiva energy awareness.

To the left of the DNA strand are representations of the seven Chakras. I created my own artistic representations of these Chakras and their Sanskrit insignia based on images I retrieved from numerous sources. The Chakras denote various centers of consciousness in Tantric Kundalini, Hindu, and other Asian systems. Briefly, the base Chakra is Muladhara and sits at the base of the spine and anus, connecting one to the Earth's energy and unconscious roots. The next Chakra, Svadhisthana, corresponds to the pelvic region, sexual organs, and bladder, the water element. Next is Manipura, the solar plexus, gut, and power function. Then appears the heart Chakra, Anahata, concerned with feelings and emotions, and is associated with the fire element. As the serpent rises, the throat Chakra, Vishuddha, is reached, representing communication, the voice, wind, and air domain. Next is Ajna, the region of vision, insight, and the third eye. The highest domain is the crown Chakra, Sahasrara, atop which sits Shiva, representing Self-realization beyond the body into the cosmic realm.

In the middle of these Chakras is seen the chemical formula of the entheogen, psilocybin. Left of the center are psilocybin mushrooms, their mycelial projections connecting to the brain (mind) extending upward to connect with the organic neurons coming from the brain that eventually neuro-link with Artificial Intelligence.

The next segment in the upper left is a typical image of a digital brain, representing Artificial Intelligence-based consciousness. As the natural world is being degraded by humans, climate change, and overpopulation, for the human species to survive, there exists the possibility that the next step in the evolution of humanity will be the extraction of consciousness from carbon-based organic matter into silicon-based inorganic states typified by supercomputers and beyond. I hope not!

Below the left-center is the wise one (Buddha) attempting to quiet the monkey-mind by encouraging the development of listening and silent observation. Looking to the right side, one will see another representation of evolution. Starting with eukaryote plankton and the invertebrate jellyfish, where life began in the ocean, it proceeds upward to a fish (vertebrate life).

To the right of each animal, an aspect of the ecosystem in which it lives is represented. As life emerges from the ocean, a frog (an amphibian) is seen adjacent to a swamp-like image. A lizard symbolizes reptilian life (and brain) in a desert setting. The eagle represents the sky animal flying in the clouds. The bear in its forest habitat stands for the evolution to the mammalian realm. The dolphin (porpoise) is the mammalian advanced intelligence of the ocean. At the bottom left hangs an abstract picture of me playing my National Steel slide guitar, representing another aspect of my creativity in music.

Note the interconnections in this piece, especially the neuronal linkage between the human brain and its artificial counterpart. In my art, I like to represent both symmetry and asymmetry, as noted between the right and left sides. Please meditate on the complex imagery and draw your own interpretations. The colors and symbols contain significant energy that I expressed in each aspect, and it is my hope you experience this energy.

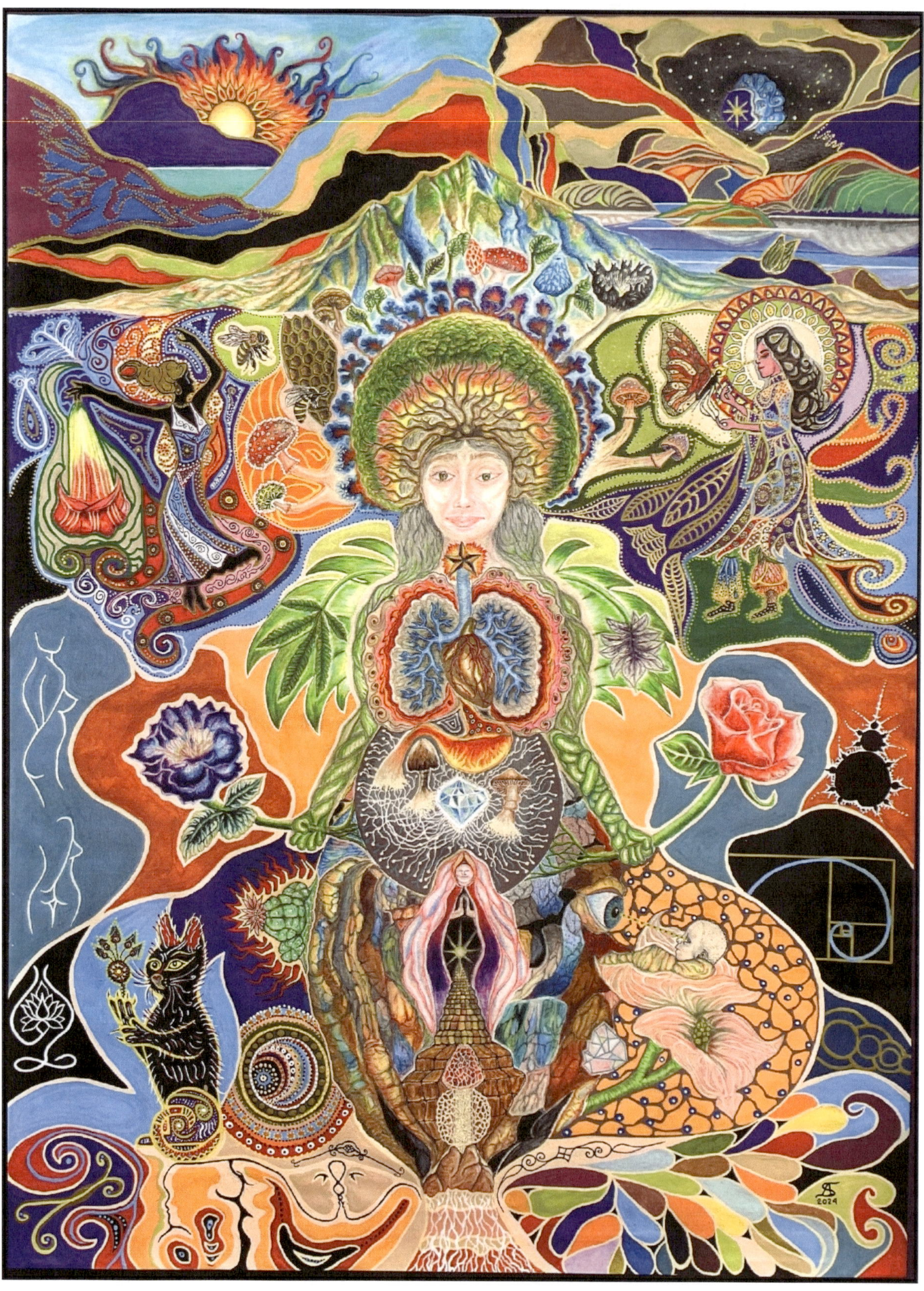

DIVINA VIRIDITAS

A vertical totem usually typifies my art to denote the main theme, and then various images are added horizontally. I started this art piece on June 1, 2024, and with a dedicated intensity, finally completed it on September 24th. It was inspired by my visionary forays into the natural world with entheogens, observation, and meditation. I name the main feminine image Divina Viriditas.

My readings about a remarkable 12th- century Catholic Abbess from Germany, Hildegard von Bingen, motivated me to honor her and the concept of *viriditas*, the greening power observed in nature. She was a polymath, contributing to the theology of her times, music, ecology, cosmology, science, poetry, ethics, mysticism, medicine, and healing arts. The patriarchal order of the church emphasized that spirituality transcended the natural world, the body, and women, thus making this oppression a sacred doctrine. Hildegard stood out as a female source of wisdom and was the first woman to be granted permission by a pope to write and preach about theology to audiences. She states that humans cannot live without nature and thus must care for all natural things. She found the Holy in the natural world and, therefore, opposed the prevailing dogma of medieval Christianity.

Hildegard coined the Latin word *Viriditas*, meaning green. This word became the prevailing force in life, emblematic of growth, fertility, and fecundity in nature. It was both a natural force and a spiritual one within humans.

Her contributions were rediscovered in the late 20th and early 21st centuries and appropriated by the ecopsychology and ecofeminism movements.

The art is not a portrait of Hildegard but a representation of the harmonious unity between the greening powers of nature and the feminine energy in all its manifestations. This includes the four elements of earth, air, fire, and water, with a tree sprouting from the woman's head, along with mushrooms, her green wings, and her holding the flowers of fertility and beauty. Dancing women, a butterfly, and bees represent pollination and joy, displaying Nature's interactive forces and manifestations.

Notice the line art displaying feminine eros on the left. On the right is the Fibonacci sequence, a mathematical truth noted in many natural objects, such as shells, human proportions, sacred geometry, and artworks. Above it is a bug-like image, an aspect of the Mandelbrot mathematical set, the origin of fractal geometry. When reiterated by a computer program, he found that a simple equation ($Z=Z^2+C$) produced incredibly complex patterns that expanded infinitely as it was generated, and this bug image was periodically reproduced. Some think this bug-like image is the mathematical imprint of the Godhead. Fractal mathematics is seen throughout the natural world (e.g., in tree branching, shorelines, and weather patterns).

As one moves downward from the face, one enters the vocal chakra, the center of communication, and then to the heart and lung energies of life (blood and oxygen). One observes digestion in the solar plexus and a mycelial network with two flowering mushrooms. The diamond represents the sacred, incorruptible power of humans and Nature. Then, one descends to the fornix, the female opening to the spiritual realm. Below is a bridal veil mushroom, the masculine element approaching the staircase to heaven, and the spiritual dimension.

To the left of the fornix is the black cat familiar, staring and playing with an object of fascination and a Peyote cactus emanating energy. On the right side is a child swaddled in a blanket held within a flower. The eye of feminine consciousness, the Great Mother, and the natural world of viriditas are being imprinted on the child. Some line art is visible at the bottom left. Look closely to see the images of two faces kissing.

My art is complex, with many spaces filled with symbols and images to incite your imagination and meditation. The colors are vivid to compensate for my red-green color deficiency and the penetrating colors observed in psychedelic journeys. My art displays energy. I focus all my psychic energy (libido) into small segments each day and later stitch them together to create the whole piece. I hope that the many hours I spend manifesting intense energy into the images will be transferred to the viewer.

Overall, this piece honors Mother Nature in her numerous manifestations and promotes the need for stewardship of our planet. Spend time contemplating the various segments depicted.

Hildegard stated, "When you see aridity, make it green." How does this quote apply to our psyche?

(A good reference: *Experiencing Hildegard: Jungian Perspectives*, Avis Clendenen.)

MANIFESTING

from the
LOST GOSPEL OF THOMAS
(32:10-11)
Discovered in December 1945
in Nag Hammadi, Egypt

"If you bring forth
what is within you,
what you bring forth
will save you.

If you do not bring forth
what is within you,
what you do not bring forth
will destroy you."

(Attributed to Jesus)

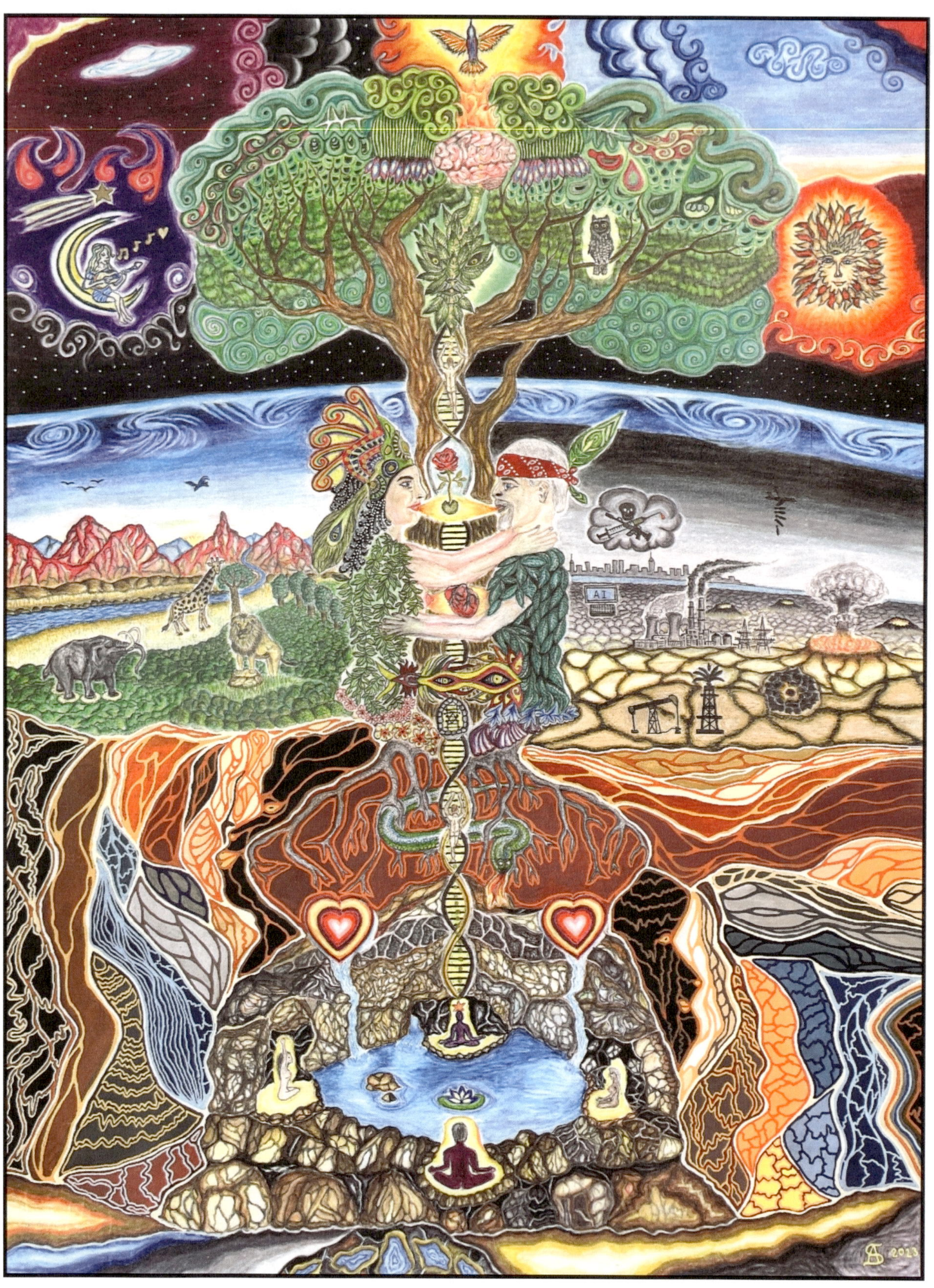

YGGDRASIL: THE SACRED TREE OF LIFE

drew this art piece from April to June 2023. Every picture tells a story; this image is a montage of several visionary journeys from the past. Visualize it as a moving, three-dimensional picture by following the various symbols depicted in the three sections of the middle, upper, and lower world, frequently explored during a psychedelic session.

The main image is the Tree of Life, which serves as the vertical axis of a shamanic experience. In Nordic mythology, this was the sacred ash tree, Yggdrasil. In the center, the Queen of Nature embraces a man, representing me. She passes a seed from her mouth to mine with a kiss, which sprouts a flower, a rose symbolizing love. The goddess asks me to plant this seed in the earth behind me to foster new growth and fertility. She says, "If indeed you love me, this is your task in life. I need a potent male to serve me, and if you do this, I will always give you my love and protection."

Middle Earth represents our daily existence. Behind the male figure is the parched earth being degraded by human intervention, depicting the consumption of non-renewable resources such as oil and coal. A nuclear power plant is polluting the air, and an atomic explosion is depicted. A computer represents the technological threat of extinction by artificial intelligence replacing carbon-based human life with virtual reality. A large gray city skyline is seen on the horizon; in a cloud above is the poison of humanity's violence, including an automatic rifle and drug abuse. In the darkening sky, a plane drops the destructive bombs of war. Hate, fear, exploitation, and lifelessness are portrayed in this scene.

Behind Mother Nature, the natural world flourishes with plant and animal life, including birds and a stream of pure flowing water. Nature tells us that the survival of humanity and the earth itself is our choice, fostered by an awareness of loving the planet.

As one enters the center of the shamanic tree, two directions are possible. One can descend below the surface to examine the roots and origin of one's life. Nourishment is provided by the richness of the soil, with all its microbes and fungi interconnecting plant life. In these roots, one recalls past memories and asks for healing and understanding of ancestral karma and pain. Descending deeper into the earth lodge, one encounters a grotto enclosing the "Well of Remembrance," where the wise meditate in their naked vulnerability. Here, one asks for wisdom to bring back to the reality of daily life. This Well also represents the "Cave of the Heart," where one joins with family, friends, ancestors, and shadow enemies to gain insight to reconcile all the split-off aspects of the psyche requiring resolution for healing and wholeness. Each of these entities is asked to speak and present their point of view. This integration brings the experience of acceptance and profound unity. Notice the ladder of DNA, which contains the genetic memories of our entire evolution. The past and present mingle.

Ascending the Tree of Life from its center, one moves beyond the sky-world and the mind to the cosmic realm of transcendence and spiritual enlightenment. Sol (sun) is depicted with his third eye of shining awareness, and Luna (moon), the reflective feminine energy, sings a beautiful song with her guitar.

The image expresses both the horizontal and the vertical planes of shamanic exploration. It also depicts the various chakra levels of awareness, from the roots where the serpent awakens with its primal power. As one proceeds upward, one passes through the genital, heart, voice, and mind chakras to eventual spiritual transcendence. Many insights are revealed by exploring these various directions leading toward wholeness. It is helpful to view this art piece from a distance and then more closely to meditate on all the symbolic expressions.

What I see in my mind's eye is far more vivid than what I can portray artistically. I worked on this for several months. I would complete a few details each day until the work was finished. Some days, I surprised myself with what manifested.

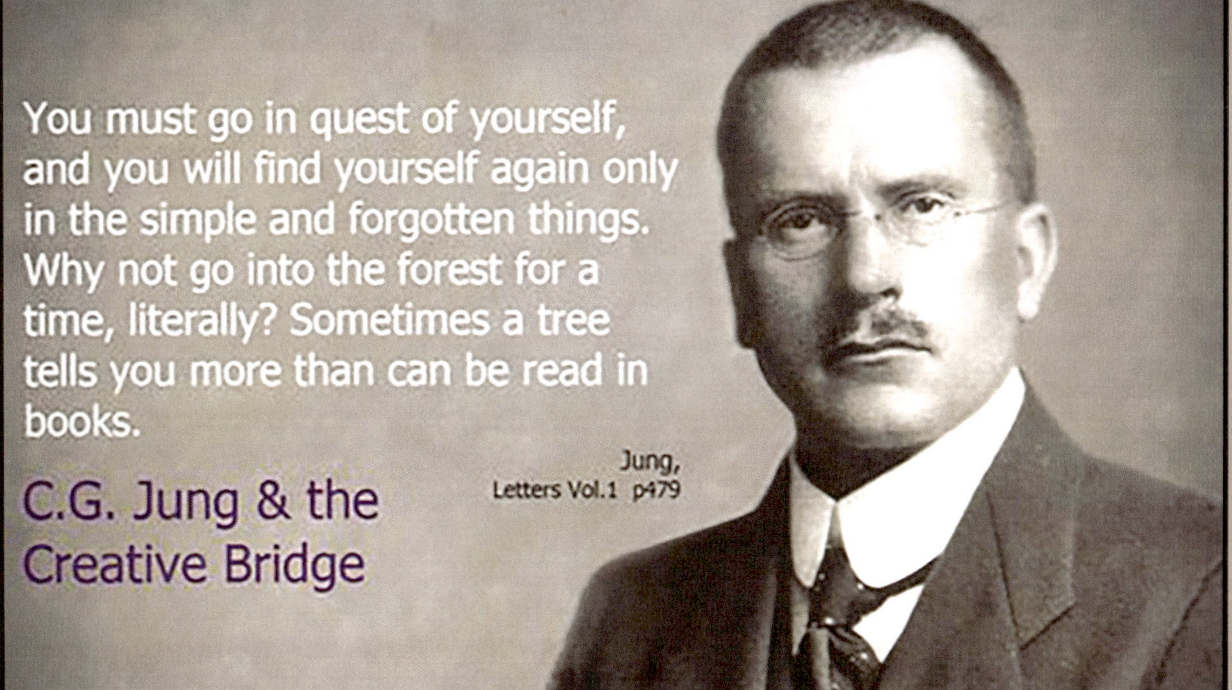

You must go in quest of yourself, and you will find yourself again only in the simple and forgotten things. Why not go into the forest for a time, literally? Sometimes a tree tells you more than can be read in books.
Jung, Letters Vol.1 p479
C.G. Jung & the Creative Bridge

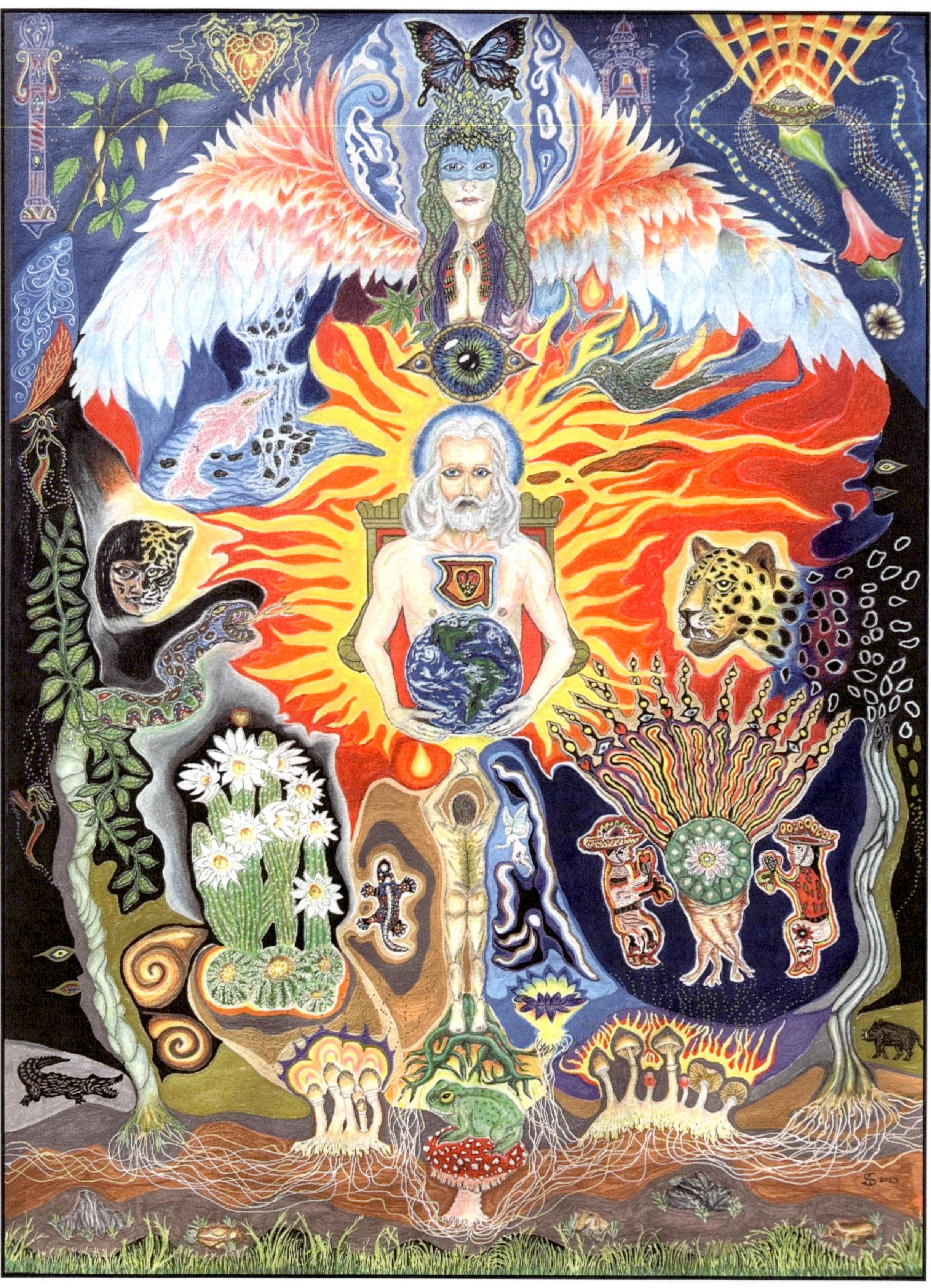

VISIONARY PLANTS MEDITATION

This static image moves as the eyes scan and meditate on the many symbolic representations. First, on the vertical axis, the old wise man, father figure, and male aspect of the godhead is envisioned, sitting on a flaming throne and holding Mother Earth, with the heart chakra icon in the center of his chest. The naked man, who symbolizes vulnerability and humility, bows before the sacred father, hoping to receive wisdom. From his feet, roots appear, entering the earth. The magic toad, Bufo alvarius, which contains the hallucinogen DMT, sits upon the sacred Amanita muscaria toadstool. To the left and right of the toad are depictions of psilocybin mushrooms emanating energy upward for inspiration and vision. Underneath the mushrooms, one sees a mycelial network representing the interconnections within the earth and connects to two images of the ayahuasca vine, Banisteriopsis caapi. These mycelia are the neural connections to other plant life and are possibly the brain of our planet communicating within the ecosystem.

On the left, the caapi vine turns into the sacred serpent of the Amazon, known as Sachamama. Intermixed are the tryptamine-containing leaves of the Psychotria viridis plant, Chacruna, the other component brewed in ayahuasca. Above the serpent, the image of a native shaman combines with the head of the jaguar; further above is the pink dolphin of the Amazon and a life-giving waterfall, often experienced in ayahuasca journeys. On the right, the vine turns into the sacred jaguar as seen in ayahuasca visions. The serpent and the jaguar are the apex predators of the jungle rainforest floor, which they protect. They can also be spirit guides imparting wisdom to participants in healing rituals. To the left of the man, a blooming San Pedro cactus, *Trichocereus pachanoi*, is seen. The visionary San Pedro cactus contains the plant medicine mescaline. On the right side is the peyote cactus, *Lophophora williamensii*, which also contains the sacred chemical mescaline, producing heart-centered visions. There are two Huichol shamans shaking rattles and praying for divine revelations, as viewed in the accompanying powerful emanations. As one proceeds upward on the vertical axis, the eye of transpersonal awareness and spiritual consciousness is observed; above it, an angelic feminine goddess is depicted with her wings spread over everything to protect the earth: all the plants, animals, humanity, and the male godhead. From her crown emerges a butterfly, the symbol of the soul. In the upper left is the iboga bush with its arabesque images as seen in visions. In the right corner is a flying saucer, which represents extraterrestrial, cosmic imagery often witnessed with ayahuasca medicine. A Brugmansia flower, Angel's trumpet, another sacred plant, emerges below. Also, a holy temple image above the wings is represented.

Various animals appear as some of my guides during these journeys and are described in detail in my book, *Visionary Healing*. The crocodile, the wild boar, and the lizard represent the more primitive and instinctual aspects of my psyche. Interspersed are several fairy images as seen during psychedelic adventures.

Overall, this artwork combines various psychedelic medicine plants that I have experienced over the years, primarily ayahuasca, psilocybin, San Pedro cactus, iboga, peyote, and the magical toad.

When I meditate on the piece, I recall many of the insights that these sacred plants bestowed upon me, allowing transformation and healing of my wounds and clarity about my destiny.

Advice from Maria Sabina, Mexican healer and poet – "Heal yourself with the light of the sun and the rays of the moon. With the sound of the river and the waterfall. With the swaying of the sea and the fluttering of birds. Heal yourself with mint, neem, and eucalyptus. Sweeten with lavender, rosemary, and chamomile. Hug yourself with the cocoa bean and a hint of cinnamon. Put love in tea instead of sugar and drink it looking at the stars. Heal yourself with the kisses that the wind gives you and the hugs of the rain. Stand strong with your bare feet on the ground and with everything that comes from it. Be smarter every day by listening to your intuition, looking at the world with your forehead. Jump, dance sing, so that you live happier. Heal yourself, with beautiful love, and always remember . . . you are the medicine."

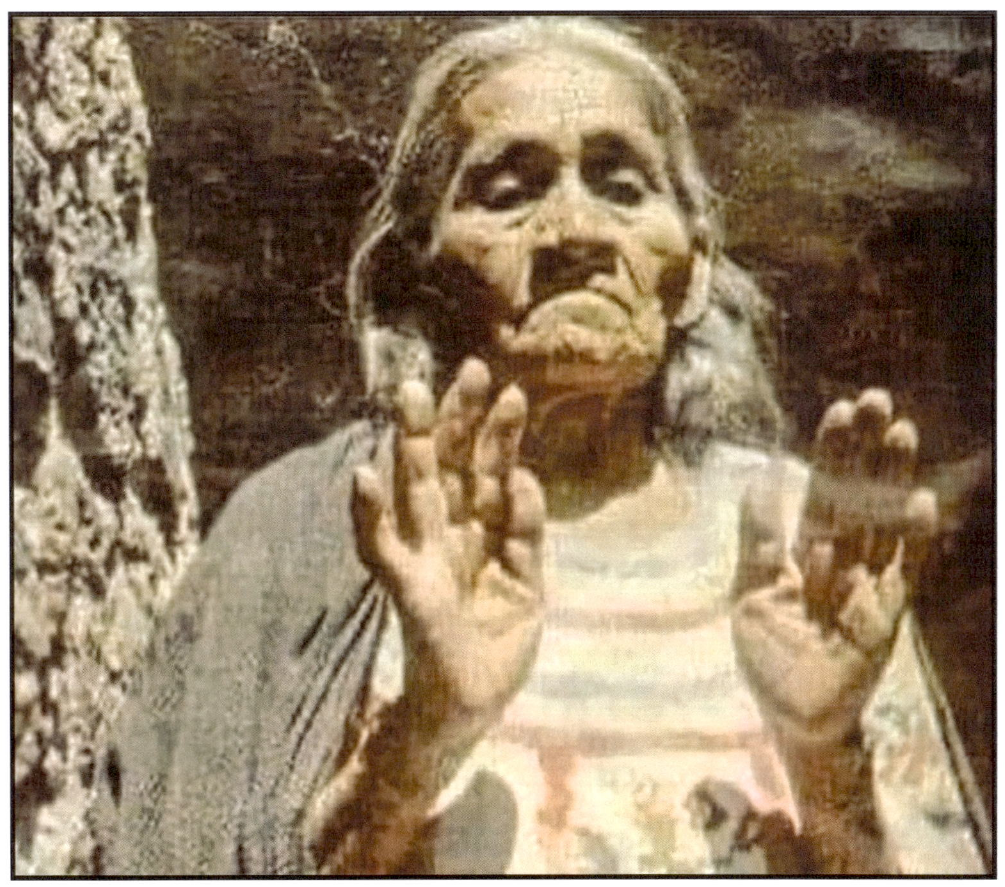

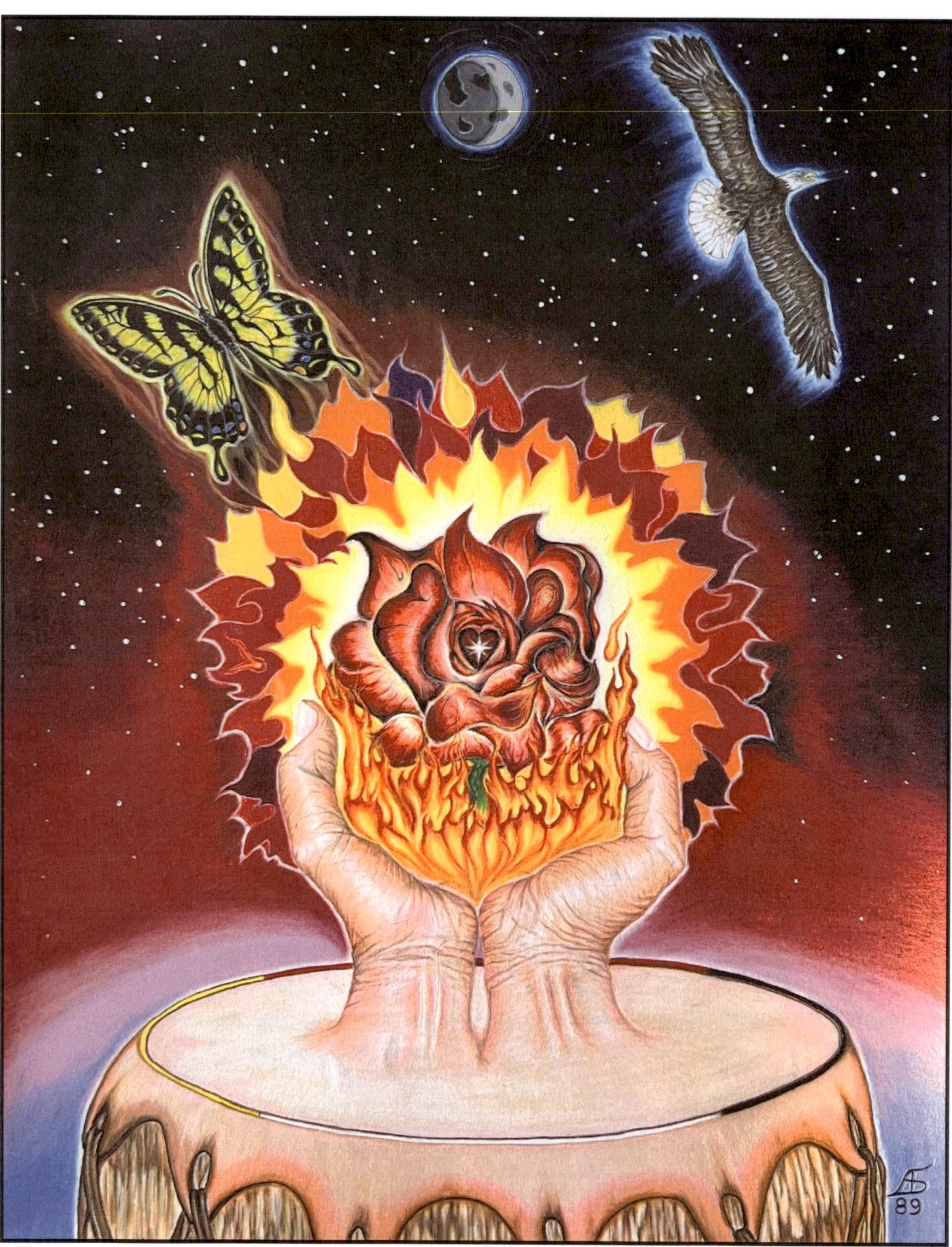

PEYOTE VISION

This image emerged from my experiences with the cactus medicine Peyote. I had the privilege of working with a Navajo Peyote Road Man named Spirit Eagle, who led ceremonies utilizing the traditional water drum, fire, cedar, sage incense, chanting, and medicine.

The image depicts cupped hands holding a fire that emerges from the shaman's drum as it beats three times per second. The rose and heart appear, expressing the feeling of universal love. Peyote is a heart-centered medicine containing the chemical mescaline. In the center shines the divine star of the Creator. Flames of divine energy emanate outward, releasing a butterfly and an eagle. The butterfly is a symbol of both the soul and the psyche. The eagle signifies the spirit soaring into the cosmos. The moon at the top denotes reflective awareness. The drumbeat is the rhythm of the universe's heartbeat and entrains the brain into a trance state.

Peyote is considered a sacrament by numerous indigenous tribes in Mexico, in particular, the Huichol Indians who live in the Sierra Madre range. The Huichols have an annual peyote hunt to collect this cactus for spiritual use by the tribe. Additionally, it is legally used by numerous Native American tribes in the United States as a spiritual sacrament by the Native American Church, which has over 300,000 adherents. Peyote was first brought to the Oklahoma territory in the late 19th century by a Commanche named Quanah Parker. When he became ill, traditional doctors were unable to help him, so the family called an Indian healer who cured him by giving him a bitter tea containing peyote and helped by chanting.

Visions from the Unconscious

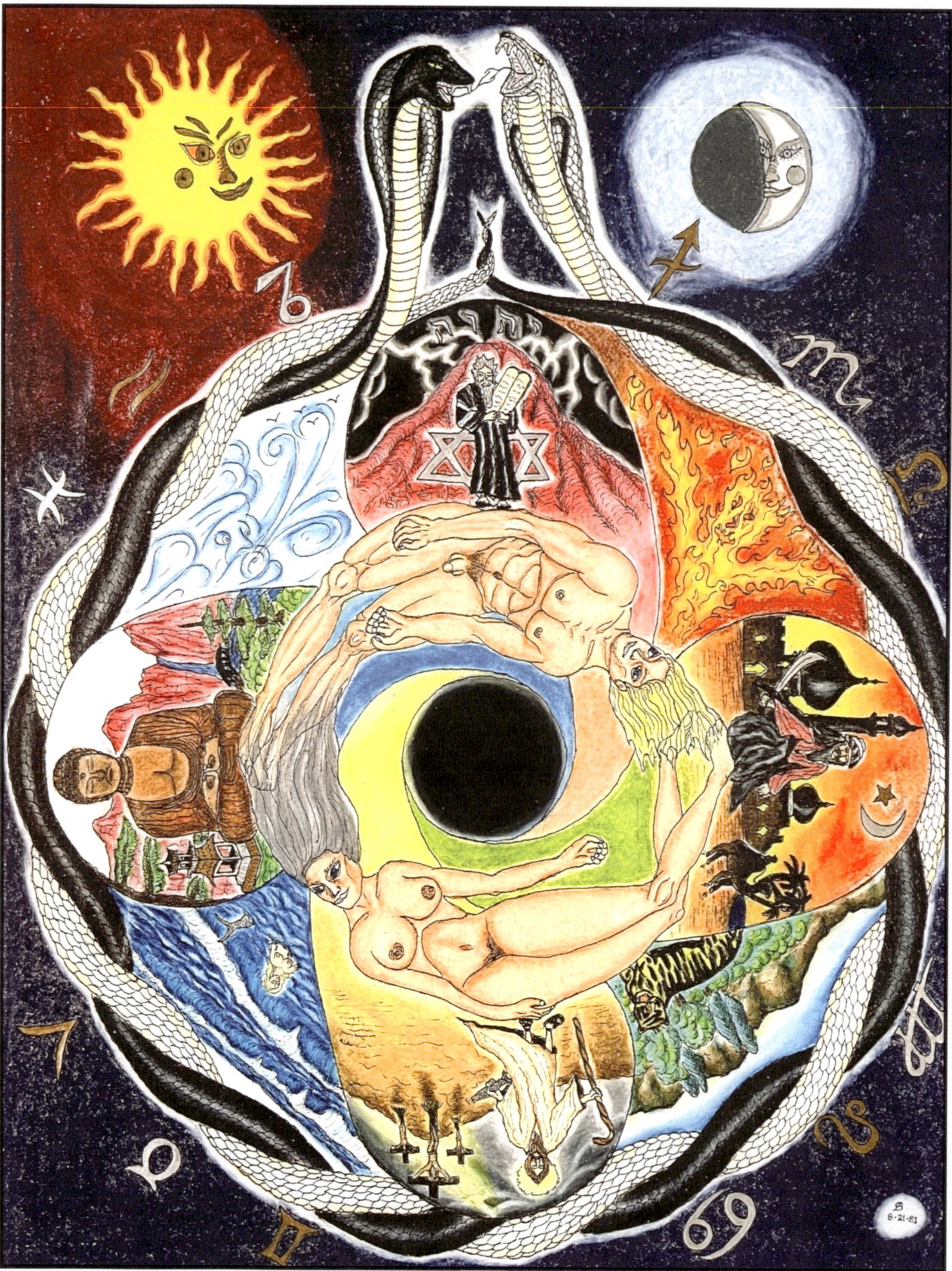

COSMOS MANDALA

I call this image the Cosmos Mandala. It represents the consciousness and existence of the universe. The center of the artwork symbolizes the primal darkness, the unknowable, or the unseen divinity before the Big Bang and space and time. This darkness is the source from which the various manifestations of reality emanate. The male and the female are portrayed, representing the dual principle, or the original Adam and Eve. Moving outward, four major religions are represented: Judaism, Islam, Christianity, and the Eastern sects, which include Buddhism and Hinduism. The four primary elements of earth, fire, water, and air also emerge. Encircling these eight attributes are the entwined dark and light serpents, symbolizing the instincts and the ongoing conflict of the opposites experienced in life, such as good versus evil.

Beyond the circle, one enters the cosmic realm. The twelve guiding astrological signs exemplify the influence of the motion of the stars and planets on the earth and humanity. At the top are Sol and Luna, the dynamic and reflective energies, the light and the dark, as a pair of opposites.

When meditating on the mandala, it is possible to experience "from where one came to where one will go," from materiality to spirit.

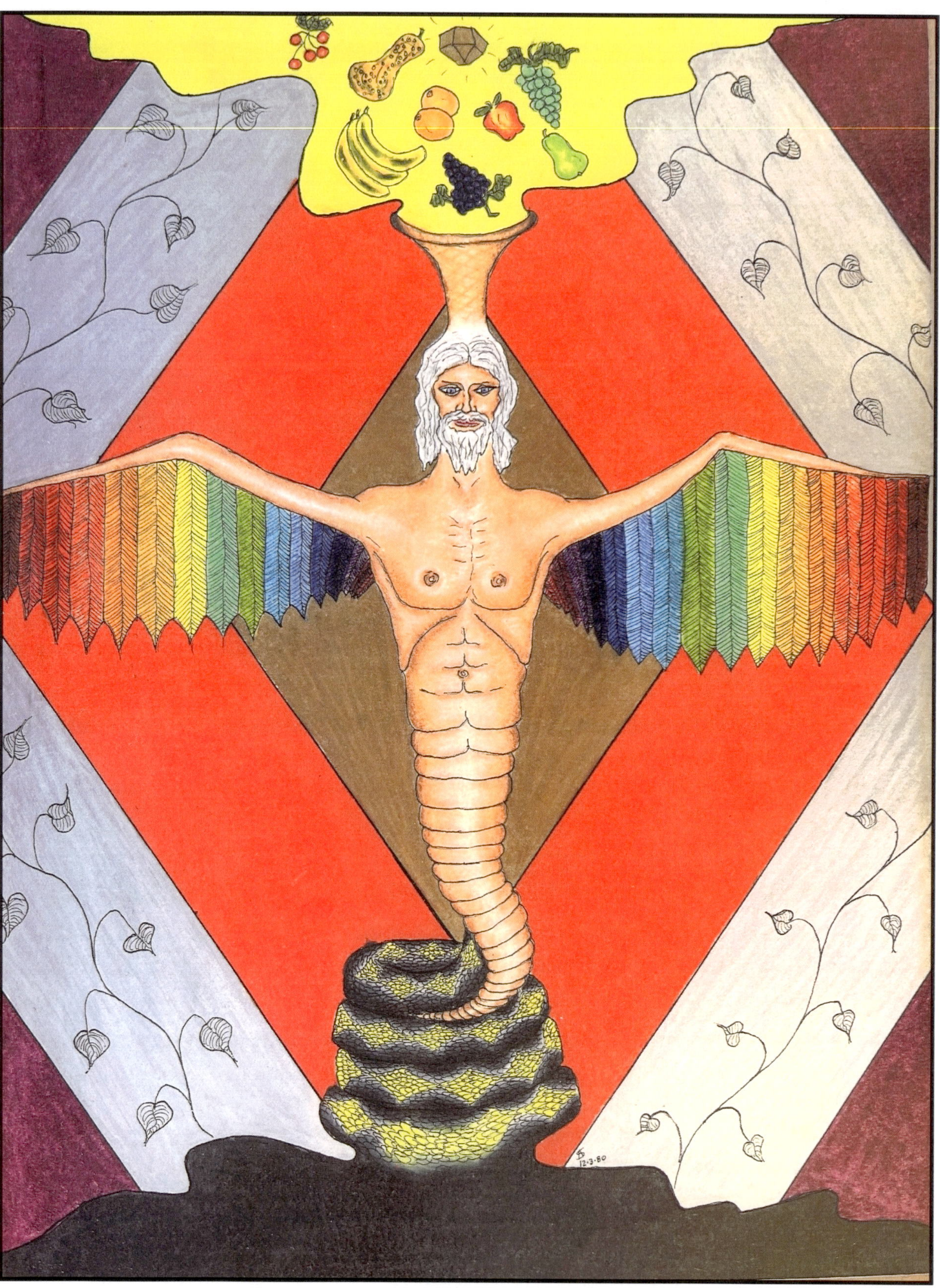

INSTINCT AND CONSCIOUSNESS

This art represents the individuation process and the evolution of consciousness that originates instinctually. The bottom of the page displays the dark, primitive, and undifferentiated nature of the unconscious, called the prima materia in alchemical symbolism. From the darkness emerges a serpent, symbolizing the awakening of instinct. The reptilian awareness then transfigures into human form and eventually into the wise man. His arms branch into wings that contain the rainbow spectrum of bird feathers, representing wholeness. Moving through the crown of this image, the fruitfulness of manifestation emerges into the light, representing the individuated human, conscious of one's destiny.

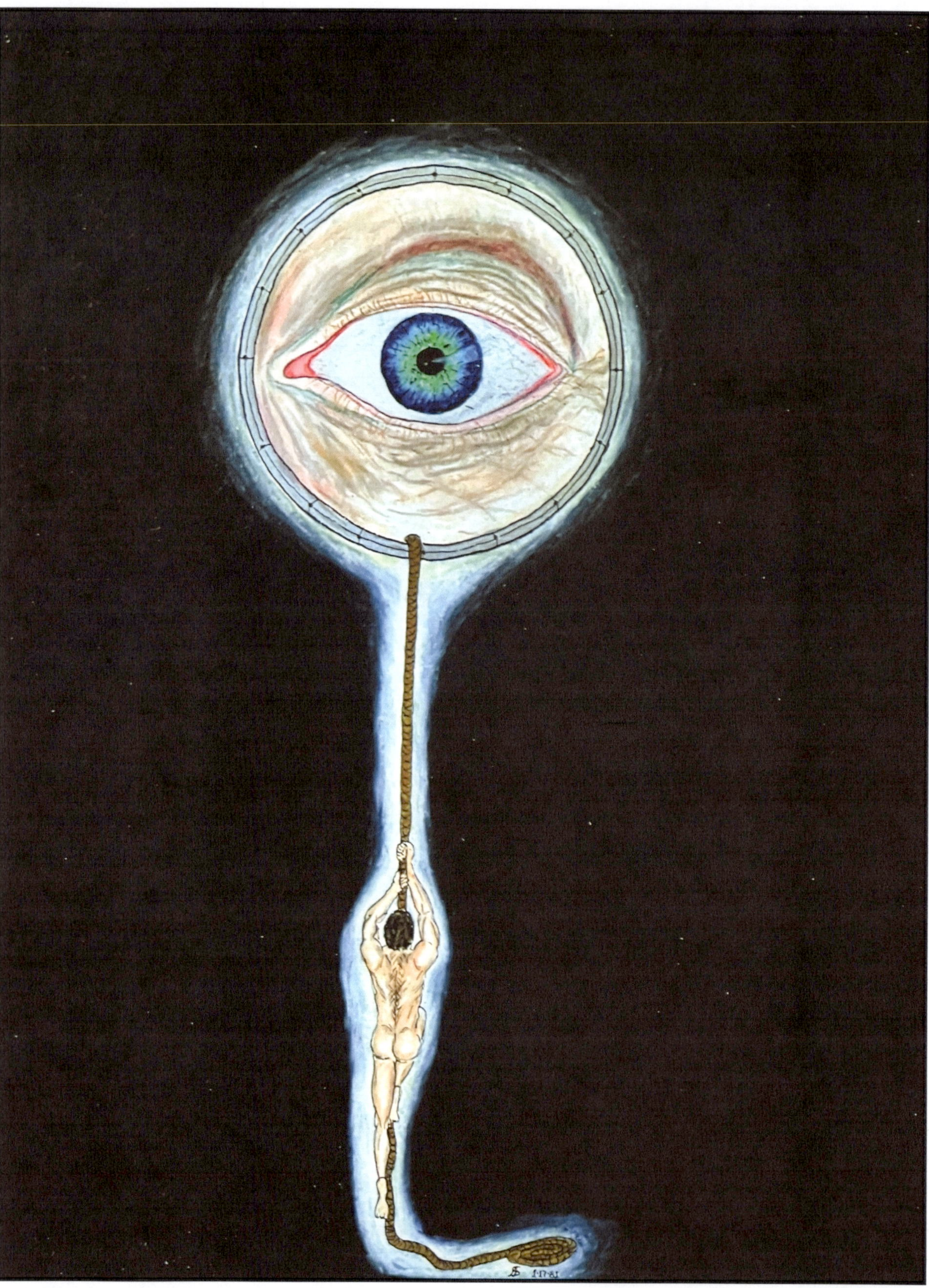

AWARENESS

What is consciousness? What is awareness?" Although these concepts are ineffable and difficult to communicate in written language, much like love, spirit, wisdom, soul, and God, they can be experienced intuitively and emotionally. Poetry better expresses the soul than prose. The eye is a symbol of awareness. The eye turned outward perceives the external world, but when turned inward, it views the soul and wisdom. It is human nature to want to be seen by someone profoundly, which validates one's existence and allows us to have an existence for others. The eye of awareness may be viewed as an image of the Godhead as one strives to see and be reflected by God. If the word God is too religious, one can call it the Divine Radiance, the Beloved, a polytheistic Nature Entity, or transpersonal intelligence.

In the Biblical story of Job, he dialogues and forms a relationship with Yahweh about the reason for his suffering despite being pious. This interchange prefigured Christ's incarnation, making God more accessible and less distant to a person. In the psychedelic experience, the ever-present observing eye(s) is a symbol that often appears.

In this artwork, the vulnerable, naked human strives to climb the rope to become more aware and to interact with the Divine. As he reaches the portal's threshold, the eye disappears as he attempts to see God face to face. However, a relationship is established when the man is seen. In the Bible, Exodus 33:20 states, "You cannot see my face, for a man cannot see me and live." Psycho-spiritually, it means that as we peer through the threshold and try to fuse with the Divine, there is an ego-death, and there is no longer a subject and object as one merges with the universal consciousness that hopefully exists in the cosmos.

One cannot relate to the Divine by aggressively seeking. It will elude the pilgrim and disappear. The Spirit can only be perceived through patience and openness to receiving it. Grace comes spontaneously to those who hunger for an inner life, often after a time of crisis or darkness.

Being seen by the Great Eye mirrors one's essence. A true lover or friend may also gaze into one's eyes, see beyond faults and imperfections, and become aware of one's soul. The Gaelic language calls this soul relationship the *Anam Cára*. When one becomes self-aware, what is observed in one's core? Is it love, or is it greed, fear, resentment, inferiority, judgment, and indifference that is perceived? Self-awareness requires endarkenment before enlightenment can occur; one must converse with these shadow aspects to heal and unify the opposites. It transforms our soul's yearnings to be understood authentically at a heartfelt level. The essence of life is to love and be loved. I prefer to call God the Beloved One.

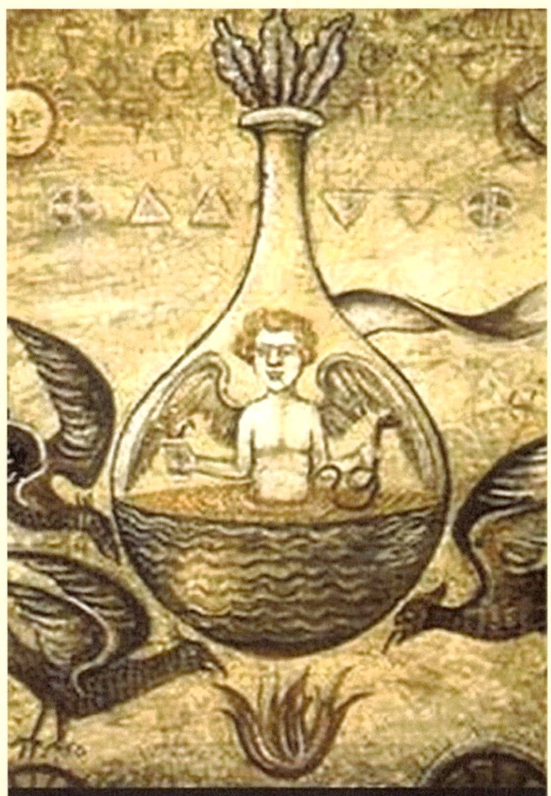

My soul, where are you ? Do you hear me ? I speak, I call you-are you there ? I have returned, I am here again. I have shaken the dust of all the lands from my feet, and I have come to you, I am with you. After long years of long wandering, I have come to you again. Should I tell you everything I have seen, experienced, and drunk in ? Or do you not want to hear about all the noise of life and the world ?

Carl Jung "The Red Book"

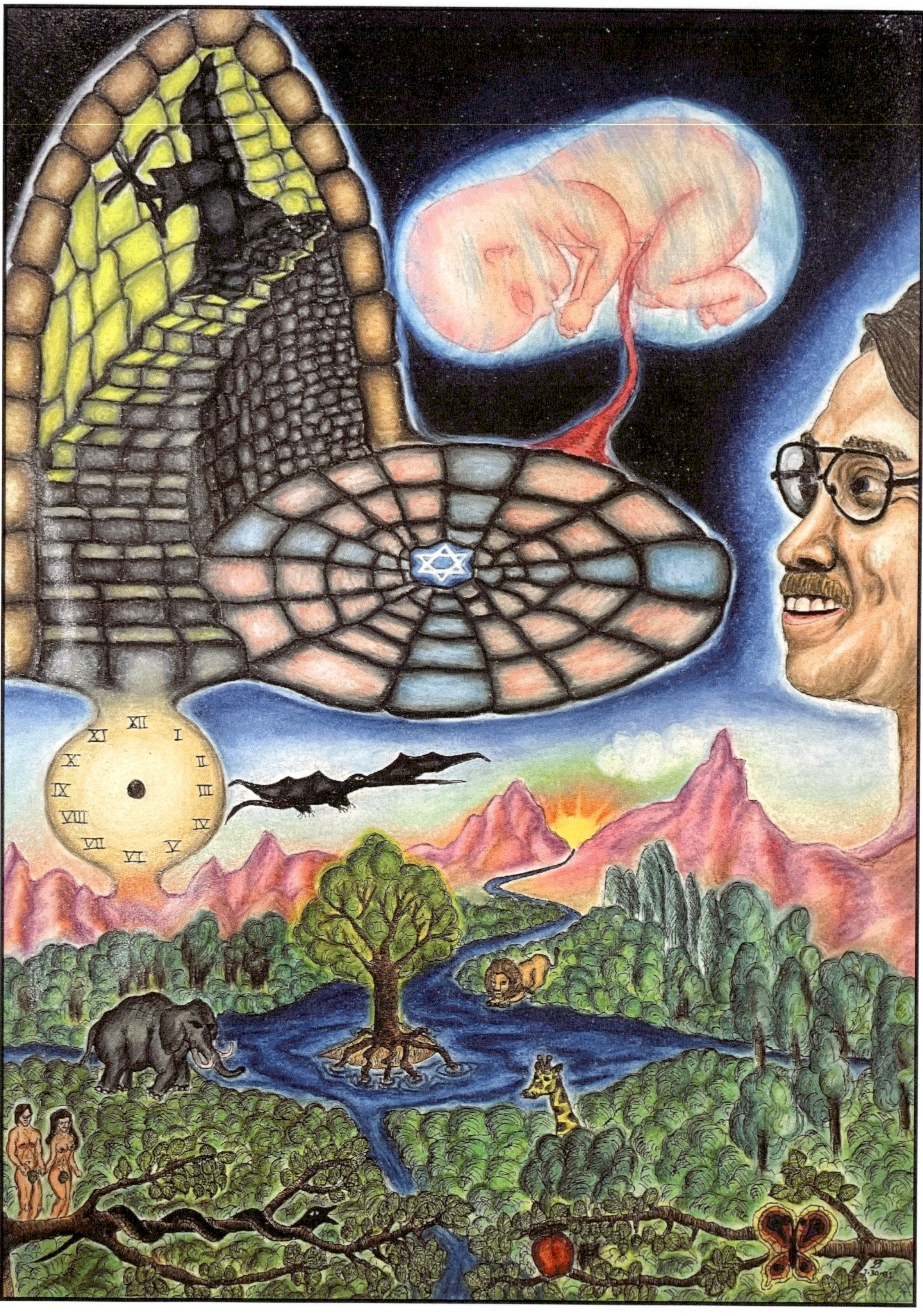

DESCENT TO THE COLLECTIVE UNCONSCIOUS

During an active imagination session, this scene emerged. The shadow of a wizard-priest appears, holding a cross as he descends a stairway in an old cathedral. He then notices a clock without hands, which indicates that he is entering a world without time, which is experienced in the unconscious realm. The soul exists in eternity and infinity beyond time and space. Below him is an ancient forest inhabited by a pterodactyl and a mammoth, representing the primeval past. A giraffe peers from the jungle, and a lion drinks from a lake fed by four rivers, representing the four directions. On the bottom left, Adam and Eve are depicted. The entire scene symbolizes the Garden of Eden, paradise, as experienced in our primordial psyche, the Collective Unconscious. In the center of the garden is the Tree of Life, with its roots nourished in a pool of water. The rising sun illuminates the new day and rebirth. Above is a tiled mandala floor with the Jewish star, symbolizing my core spiritual identity. From it emerges a developing fetus in the womb, representing rebirth, new insights, hope for the future, the radiant child, and my descendants.

Eros and Nature

MERLIN AND LADY NYNEVE

When Merlin saw the Damsel Nyneve, whom Sir Pellinore brought to court, he knew his fate was on him, for his heart swelled like a boy's heart in his aged breast, and his desires overcame his years and his knowledge. Merlin wanted Nyneve more than his life, as he had foreseen. He pursued her with his wishes and would not let her rest. And Nyneve used her power over the besotted old Merlin and traded her company for his magic arts, for she was one of the damsels of the Lady of the Lake and schooled in wonders.

Merlin knew what was happening to him and knew its fatal end, and still he could not help himself, for his heart doted on the Damsel of the Lake.

He went to King Arthur and told him that the time he once spoke of had come and that his end was not far off ... "You will miss me and wish for my advice."

"This is beyond my understanding," said the king. "You are the wisest man alive. You know what is preparing. Why do you not make a plan to save yourself?"

And Merlin said quietly, "**Because I am wise, in the combat between wisdom and feeling, wisdom never wins.**"

And he rode with Nyneve from the court ... knowing her power over him. Nyneve grew bored and restless with Merlin panting after her, begging her to lie with him and stanch his yearning ... Then Nyneve, with the inborn craft of maidens, began to question Merlin about his magic arts, half promising to trade her favors for his knowledge ... Merlin showed her many wonders, and when at last he found that he interested her, he showed her how the magic was accomplished and put in her hands the tools of enchantment, gave her the antidotes of magic against magic, and finally, in his aged folly, taught her those spells which cannot be broken by any means. And when she clapped in maidenly joy... he created a room under a great rock cliff of unbeliev-able wonders ... for the consummation of their love... but Nyneve leaped back and cast a spell that cannot be broken by any means...and the passage closed for all time to come. She could hear his voice faintly through the rock, pleading for release. And Nyneve mounted her horse and rode away. And Merlin remains there to this day, as he knew he would be.

(Excerpted from *The Acts of King Arthur and His Noble Knights*, by John Steinbeck, pgs. 99 – 101.) This myth rep-resents the eternal conflict between Logos and Eros.

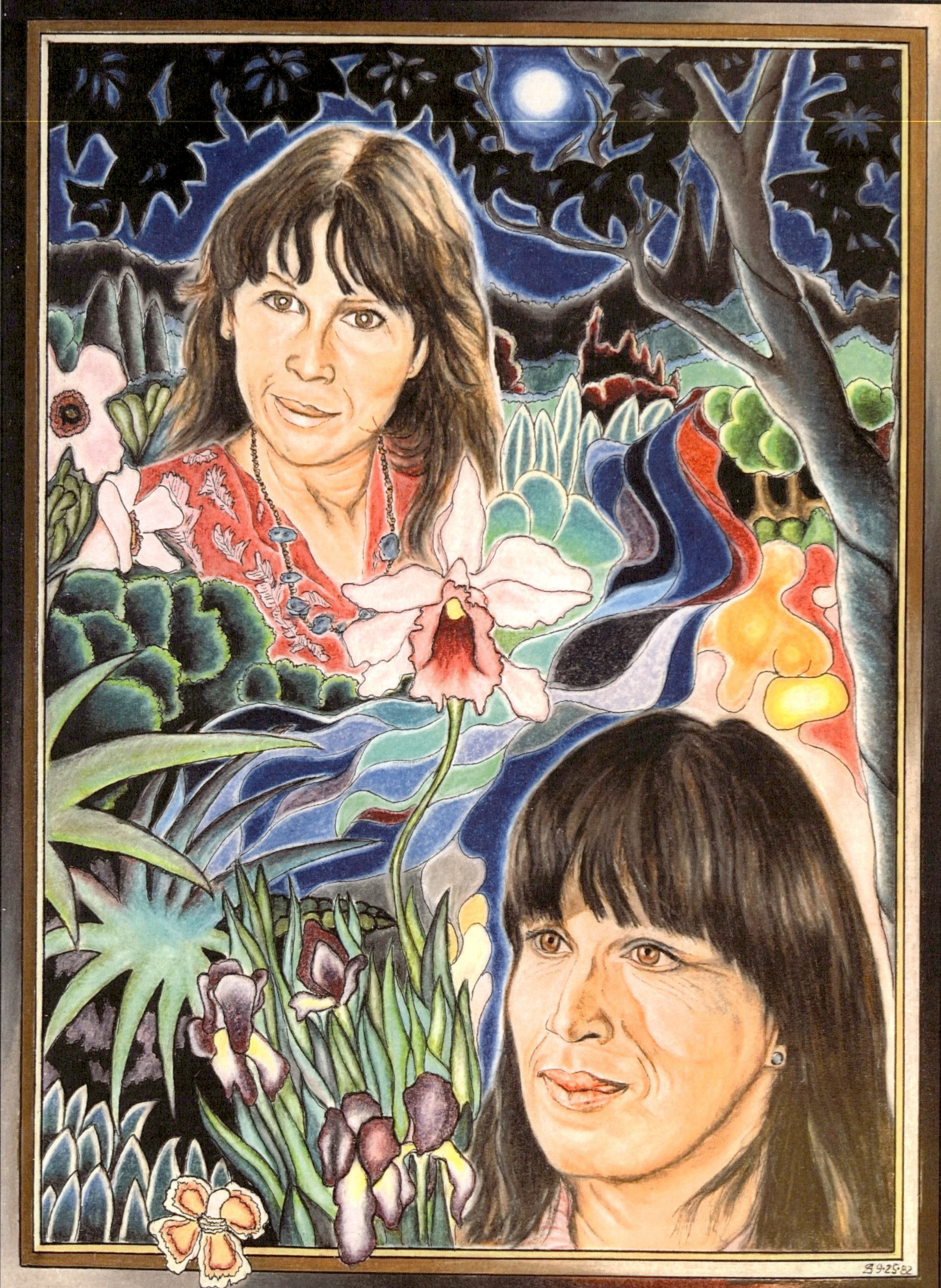

THE LOVER THROUGHOUT ALL TIME

This image depicts the beauty of the wise woman, the goddess ener-gy within the natural world. The alluring and sensual aspects of the natural world are intertwined, evoking one's desire to respect and protect the earth. On an archetypal level, she represents a timeless lover whose soul exists in eternity. In Jungian psychology, she symbolizes the anima, or feminine archetype within a man, and is often experienced as a Muse for creative inspiration. She embodies love, nurturing, and preser-vation of planet Earth and only seeks to be appreciated and respected for all her abundance and power. If exploited, her negative aspect will mani-fest, leaving one feeling abandoned, barren, and without hope.

When the anima is projected onto an actual woman, it can lead to misguided love affairs and disrupt meaningful relationships. Her arche-typal meaning as a "lover throughout all time" can become confused with the personal dimension of a committed relationship. It is essential to dis-tinguish between the two to avoid chaos, pain, and loss. When seduced by this eternal feminine, it is crucial to remember who is waiting at home and who has been there caring for you over time. Personal love must be cherished and cultivated. The same applies to a woman whose inner male side is the animus.

The Arthurian legend of Merlin and Lady Nyneve exemplifies this theme.

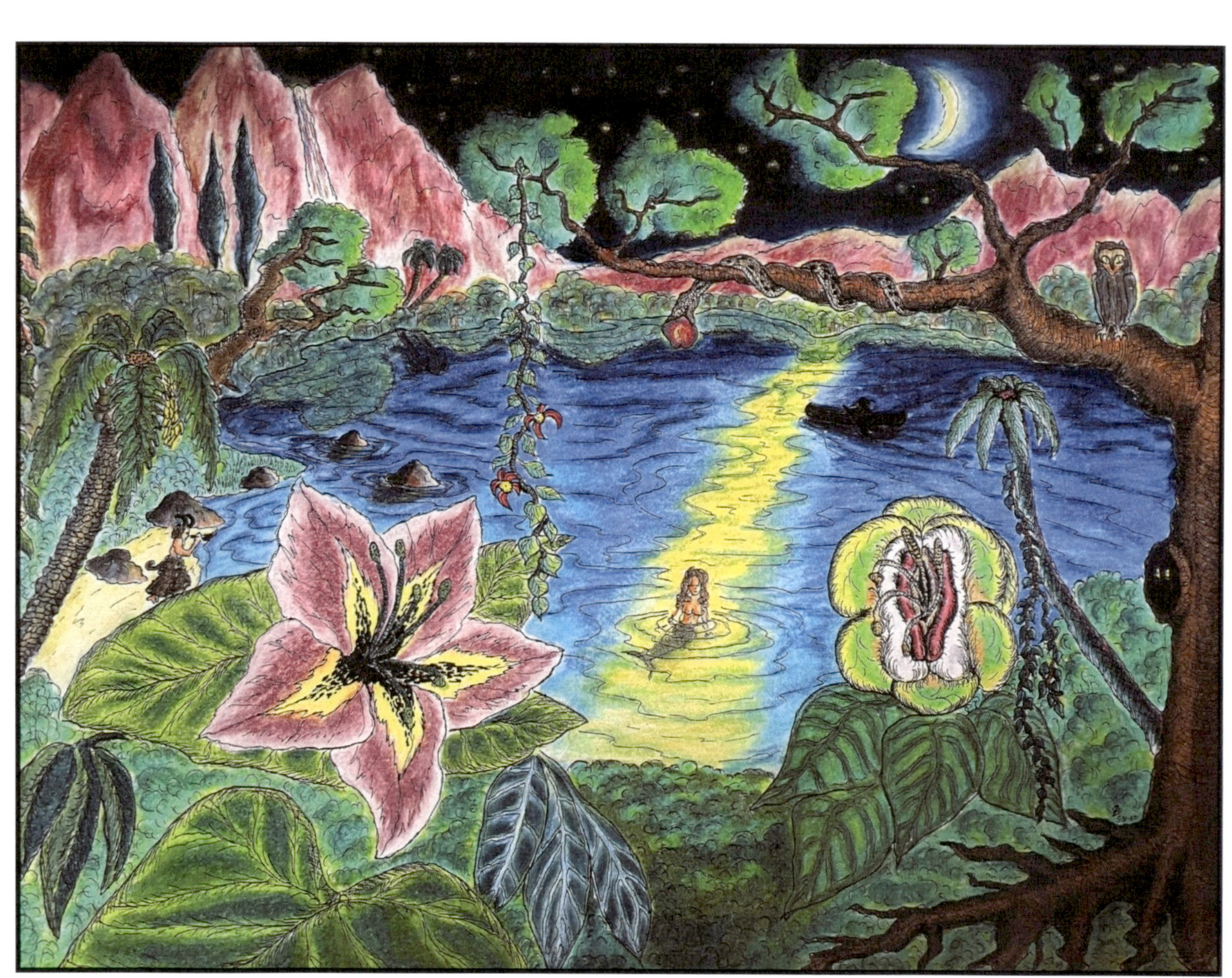

WARNING

Some of the following images may be disturbing to view for adults and are not suitable for children (under the age of 40). Many of the images from the past are primitive as I self-learned how to draw and express my inner life through art. We all go through difficult times in life, and I am no different. I came through it.

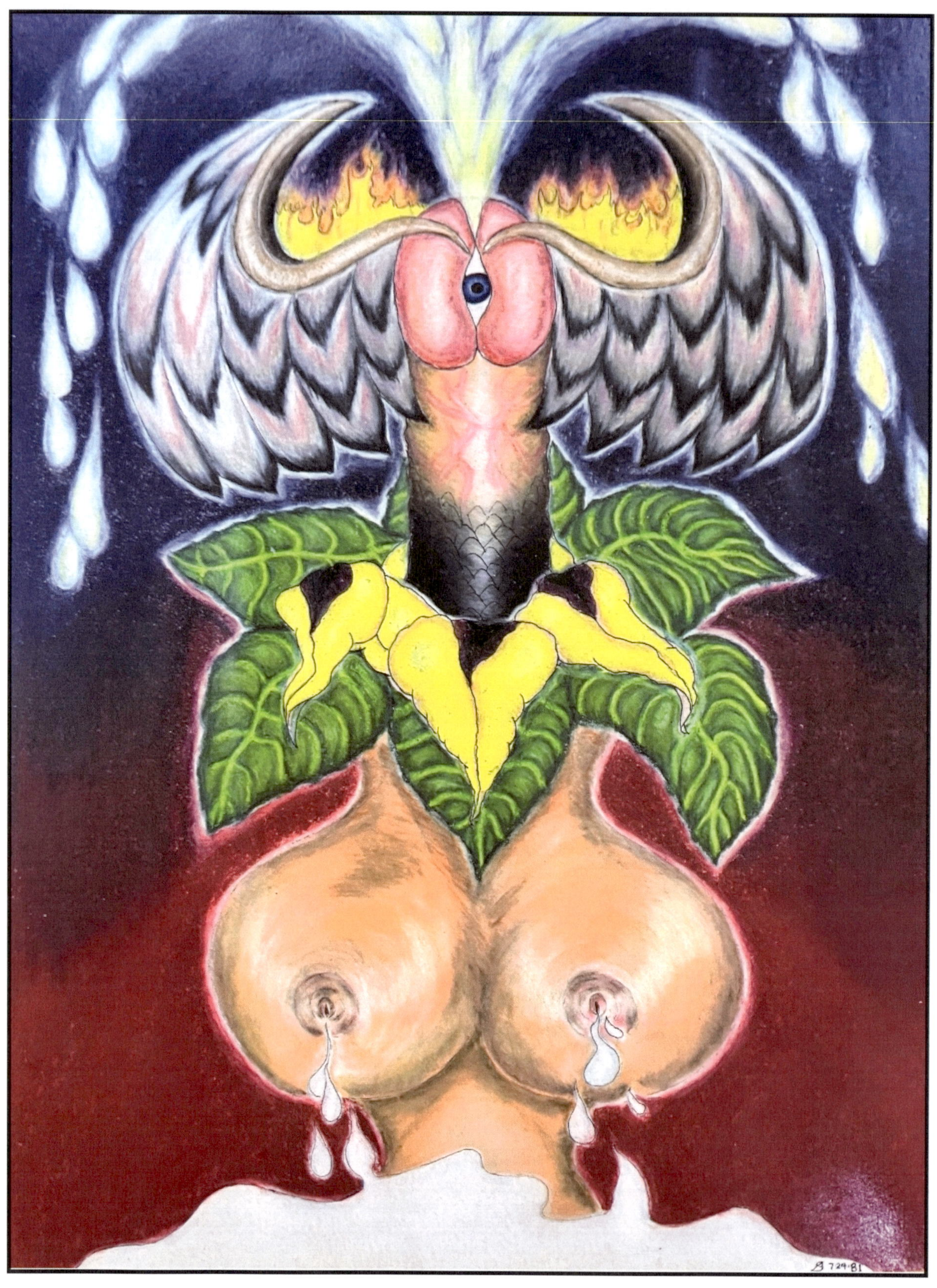

EROS AND NATURE

n my visionary experiences, I became aware that nature is sensual, not in a sexual sense, but associated with Eros, the goddess of love in Greek myths. In psychology, eros is the binding force that creates unity and connectedness. Its cosmic aspect is the force of gravity between two entities, and its personal attribute is love.

In nature, eros can be seen as the energy that brings fertility and creates new life. It generates sustainability within nature's ecosystems through adaptation, symbiosis, mutualism, and cooperation of numerous species necessary for survival. One can observe eros in the pistil, the female-bearing seed organ of a flower, and the stamen, the pollen-bearing filament, the male component of the flower. As one strolls through the natural world, one can appreciate this ever-present cycle of life and death in the plants and animals we perceive as the seasons change. In the natural world, time is circular, not linear.

The guilt a human being feels as we are made aware of our part in the degradation of the earth will not change the collective psyche toward stewarding the planet. The most effective way to change our attitudes and values toward preserving nature is through the experience of love for the earth. A positive transformation may occur when this eros is experienced within the hearts and souls of a critical mass of the human population.

The two artistic images express the fertile element of nature. The first picture displays the sensual aspects of the flowers, the mermaid, and the goat-footed and seductive Pan. The lushness in the vegetation, the reflective moon upon the water, the serpent with an apple, the eyes of the wise owl, and the peering eyes of observation in the tree reveal both the beauty and the appreciation of nature.

While the second image may seem more overtly sexual, my intention is to represent the potent masculine and the nurturing feminine instinctual forces within the animal and plant realms of the natural world, which are life-giving. It is necessary to spend time in nature to observe the interplay of the local ecosystem and various species directly and understand the concept of eros in the natural world. This eros fosters one's love of the earth, and this appreciation of the natural world becomes the key to humanity's participation in maintaining and stewarding the planet.

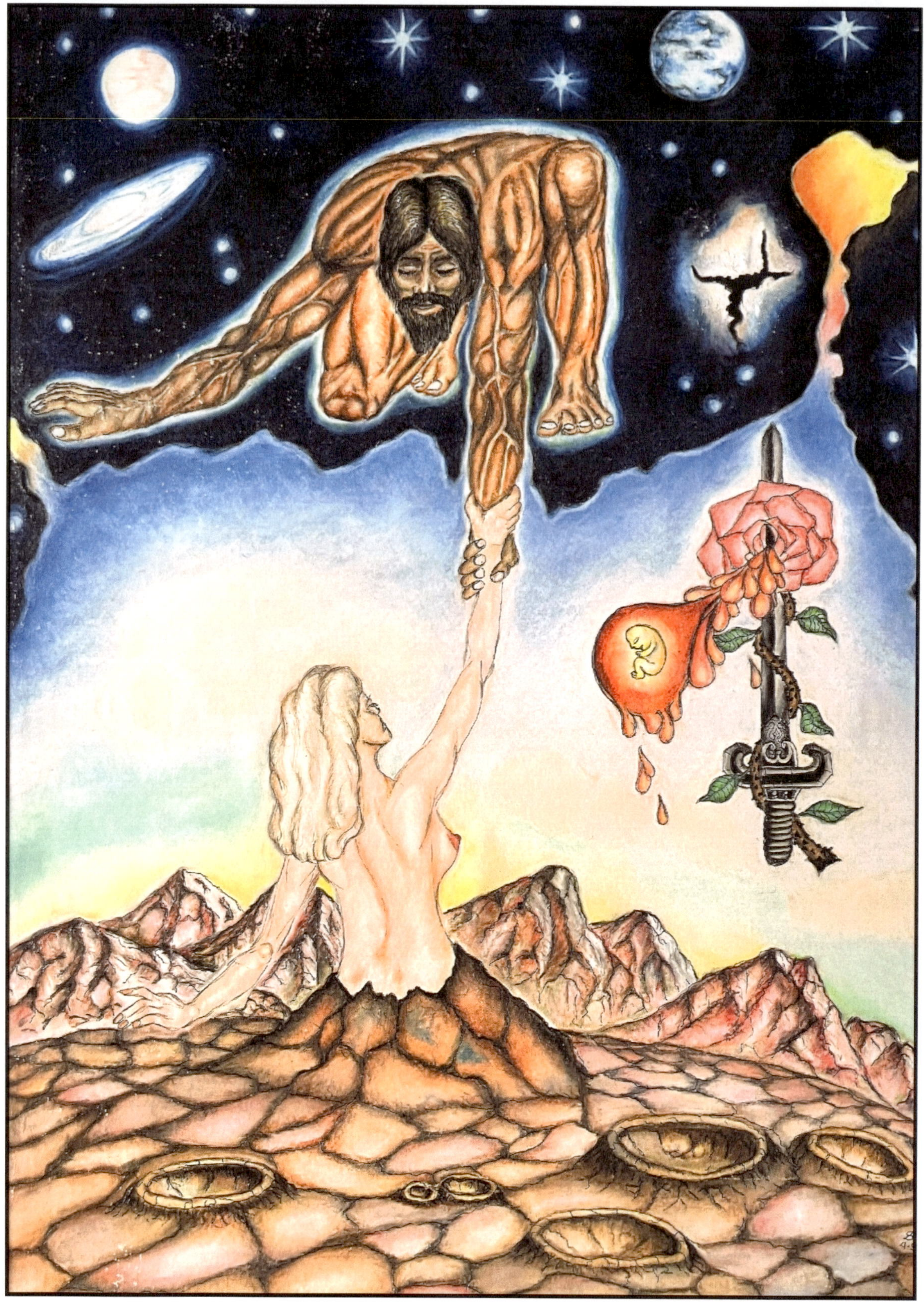

REDEMPTION OF THE FEMININE

This image was inspired by my philosophical, poetic, and art mentor, William Blake, who lived from 1757 to 1827. It was entitled "The Ancient of Days." The picture depicts a strong man residing in the cosmic, spiritual realm. He is reaching down, extracting a beautiful woman buried in the depths of the parched and neglected earth. The grip represents the union of the male and female, the spiritual and material aspects of the psyche. This union expresses the necessity of redeeming the buried, unconscious feminine energy for integration into the male psyche to create wholeness. The restoration of the natural world necessitates this conjunction to end the destruction and exploitation of the planet through male dominance by the patriarchy. It also signifies the ascension of the Goddess as a spiritual equal to a male God. The sword represents the male warrior power principle uniting with the rose, symbolizing the female eros aspect. In Greek mythology, this is portrayed by the marriage of Ares, the God of War, with Aphrodite, the Goddess of Love. It also represents the union of strength and love. This coniunctio manifests the emergence of divine birth, as seen within the womb.

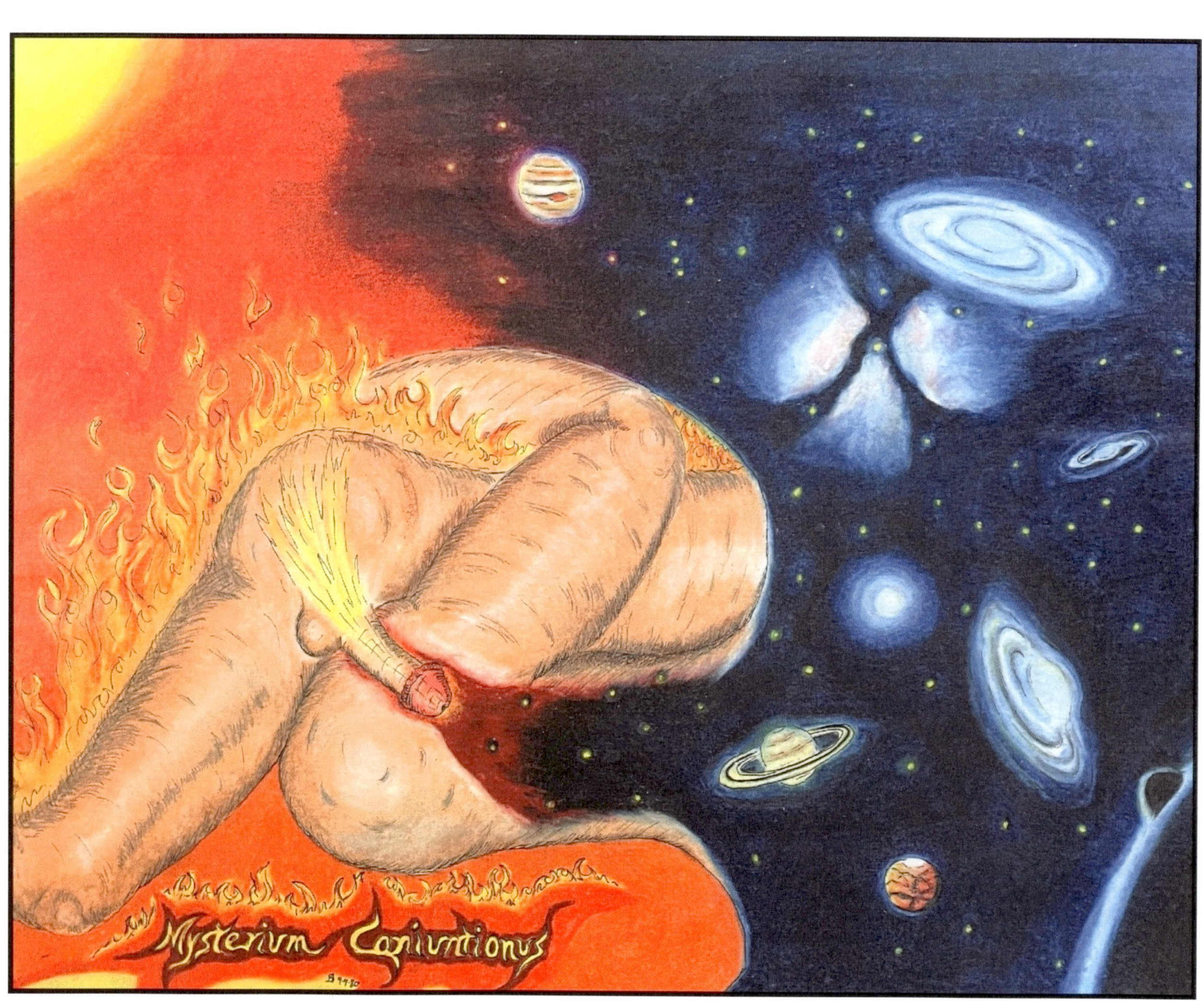

Mysterium Coniunctionus

MYSTERIUM CONIUNCTIONIS

Mysterium Coniunctionis is volume 14 of C.G. Jung's Collected Works. This book is considered his original alchemical text, rich with symbolism and challenging to read. Coniunctio means the union of opposites, a conjunction that takes the dual, disparate, differentiated, and often divisive aspects within the psyche and brings them together to form a unity. Often, it is symbolized as the sexual union of male and female accompanied by the birth of a divine child or new insights.

The image represents eros as the gateway to spirit. From an instinctual interpretation, it is a sexual experience with the male fiery element penetrating the receptive female. Sexuality, based on consensual love, is more than instinctual gratification or lust. The experience may be an entrance to the cosmic realm beyond the body, the spiritual aspect that can be experienced during sexual intimacy between two people as practiced in Tantric sexuality. An illustration from an alchemical treatise, the Rosarium Philosophorum (1550), which portrays the coniunctio (coitus) of the King and Queen, follows.

CONIVNCTIO SIVE
Coitus.

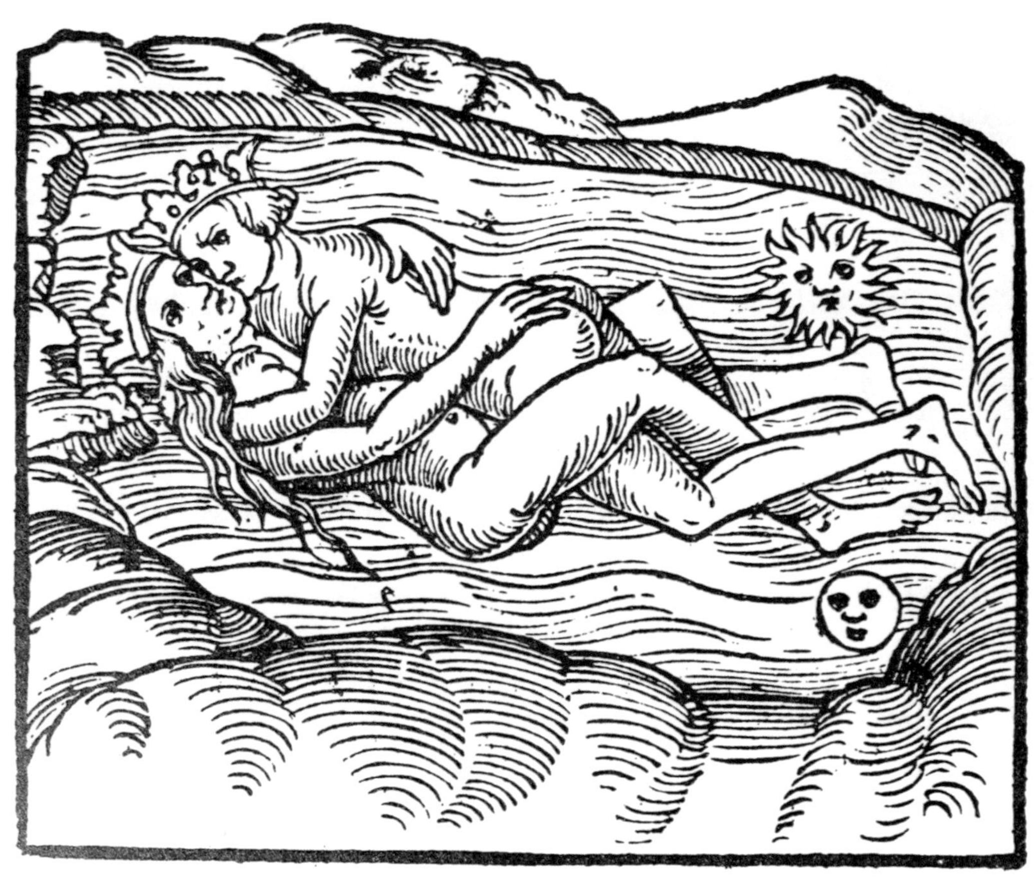

Rosarium Philosophorum — Alchemical Text

Darkness and Light

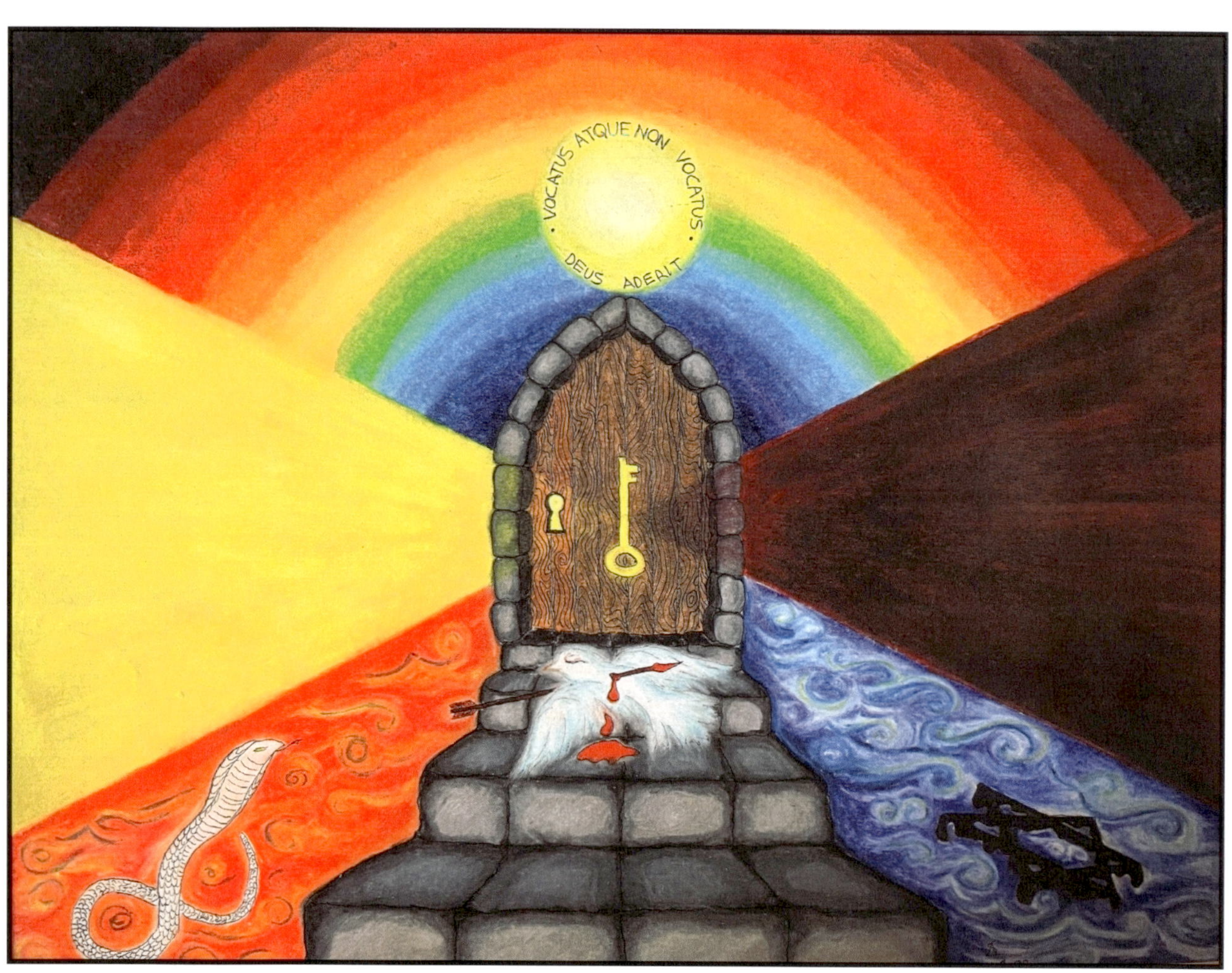

VOCATUS ATQUE NON VOCATUS
DEUS ADERIT

THE PORTAL

This image portrays a spirit bird who is wounded and disillusioned with the traumas encountered in the material world and is lying at the steps of a closed doorway. Beyond this portal is seen the intersection of light and dark, representing the duality experienced during one's lifetime. The rainbow symbolizes unity and hope, which emerges after a storm or conflict. Above the door is a Latin quote originally attributed to the Oracle of Delphi. "Vocatus Atque Non Vocatus Deus Aderit" translates to "Called or not called, God will be there." It is inscribed over the doorway of Carl Jung's home in Kusnacht, Switzerland, and means that the Divine is present, whether one believes in it or not.

The portal with the key is symbolic of unlocking the treasures of the transpersonal realm, where one can interact with the archetypes and Divine Intelligence. It also includes healing the spirit and soul and envisioning one's karmic trajectory in this lifetime. One must surrender the ego (ego death) to pass through the portal to the other side. Crisis always creates opportunity.

On the right side of the image floats a Jewish star tarnished by my cynical attitude toward my religion of origin, requiring the revitalization of my spiritual core identity. On the left is seen the instinctual power of the white serpent as it invigorates life and survival. Despite all of life's travails, the image suggests hope.

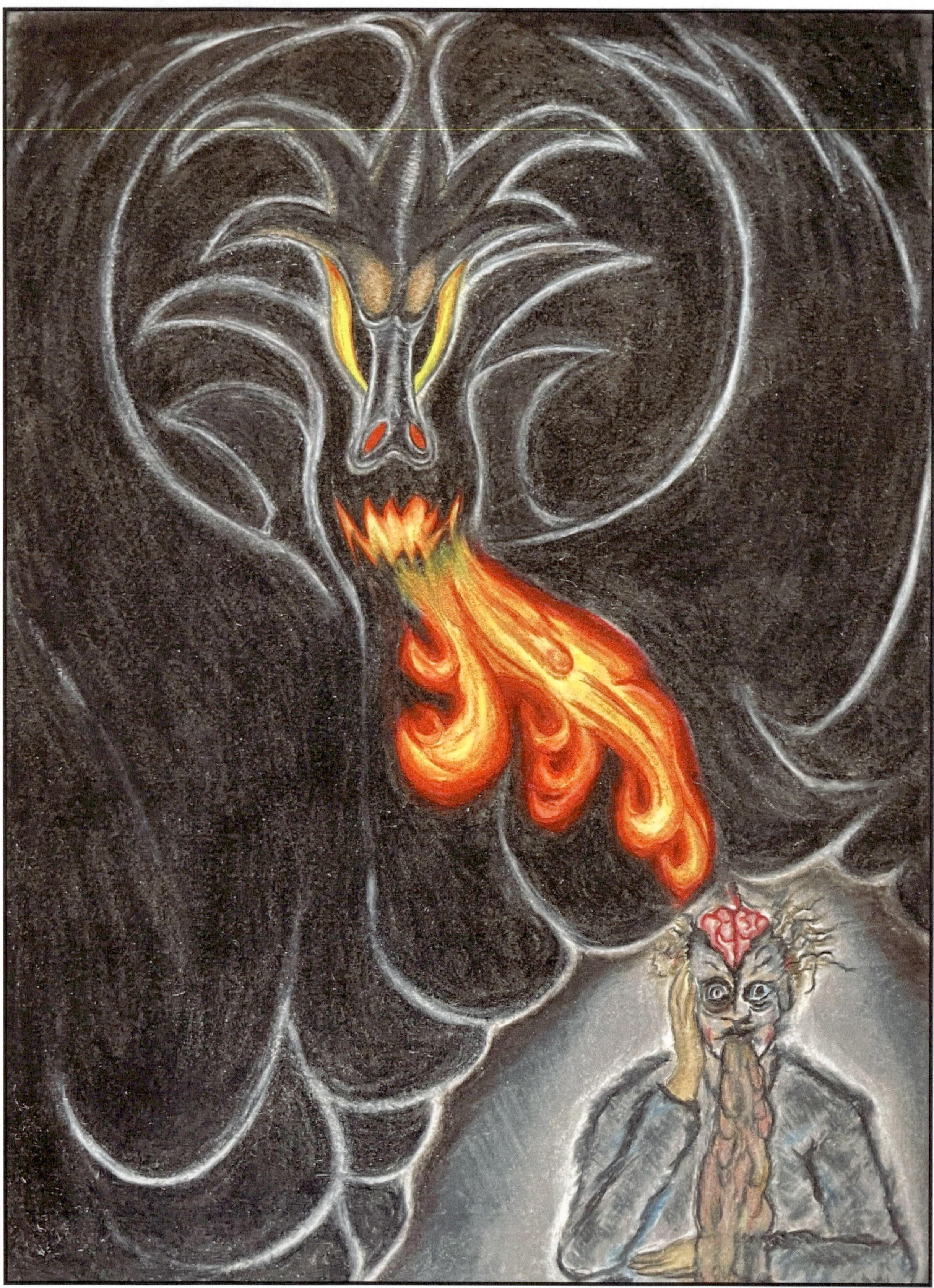

DEPRESSION

This image of darkness depicts the horror of serious depression that I witnessed with many of my patients. Unfortunately, I also experienced a significant depression in my late thirties. Here sits a discombobulated man with a fried brain (psyche) exposed to the dark and fiery forces above. The image portrays a man vomiting from the nausea of dysphoria and dressed in drab grey clothing. Art can be a great catharsis for depression and often helps beyond words.

Often precipitated by a significant loss, trauma, failure, or genetic predisposition, the clouds of darkness are ever-present as the depressed person sits isolated from the bustling, living world outside. Suicidal thoughts can enter the mind, and sleep deprivation or excessive somnolence may prevail. A struggle between the forces of the life instinct and the death instinct takes place. If one chooses suicide, the hope is that all the psychic and physical pain will end, but there is still a great mystery surrounding death. Will it release one from the unremitting agony of life by total annihilation and obliteration of consciousness, or is it possible that the soul and its suffering will continue into an afterlife realm? Thankfully, most depressed people choose to live and work to improve their mood. Darkness can be a great teacher of wisdom if one can eventually transcend it. In my practice as a psychiatrist, a patient's suicide has lasting effects on family and friends, and it has been very traumatic for me to experience as a doctor.

Healing my depression gave me an intuitive window into the dynamics of my patients. Images of light and pats on the back cannot cheerlead a person out of a depression. Images of darkness can help a patient know that I understand their experience, but ultimately, one must strive for the light to prevail.

The Italian author Dante Alighieri completed his poem, *The Divine Comedy,* around 1321. Here, Virgil guides Dante as he enters the Inferno, an allegory about hell or the experience of depression. Virgil resembles the modern therapist steering a person through darkness. Another guide, Beatrice, eventually leads Dante up to Purgatorio and, through her divine revelation, eventually to Paradiso. Endarkenment must first be integrated before spiritual enlightenment is attained. As a psychiatrist, I could lead my patients through their depression. However, my spiritual mindfulness was necessary to encourage them to ascend to a state of higher functioning, contentment, and a taste of happiness.

Healing can take place through various forms of psychotherapy and with the use of antidepressant medication. Returning to functionality and relatedness becomes a goal. When traditional treatments do not work, alternatives require consideration. Newer treatments with psychedelic medicines and ketamine are now being researched and used to treat patients with resistant depression.

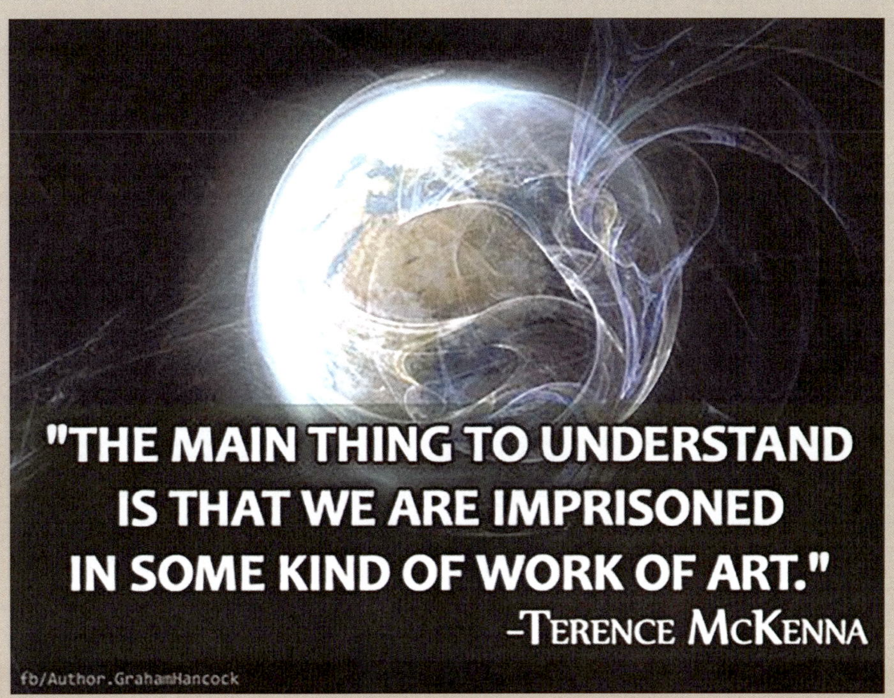
"THE MAIN THING TO UNDERSTAND
IS THAT WE ARE IMPRISONED
IN SOME KIND OF WORK OF ART."
-TERENCE MCKENNA
fb/Author.GrahamHancock

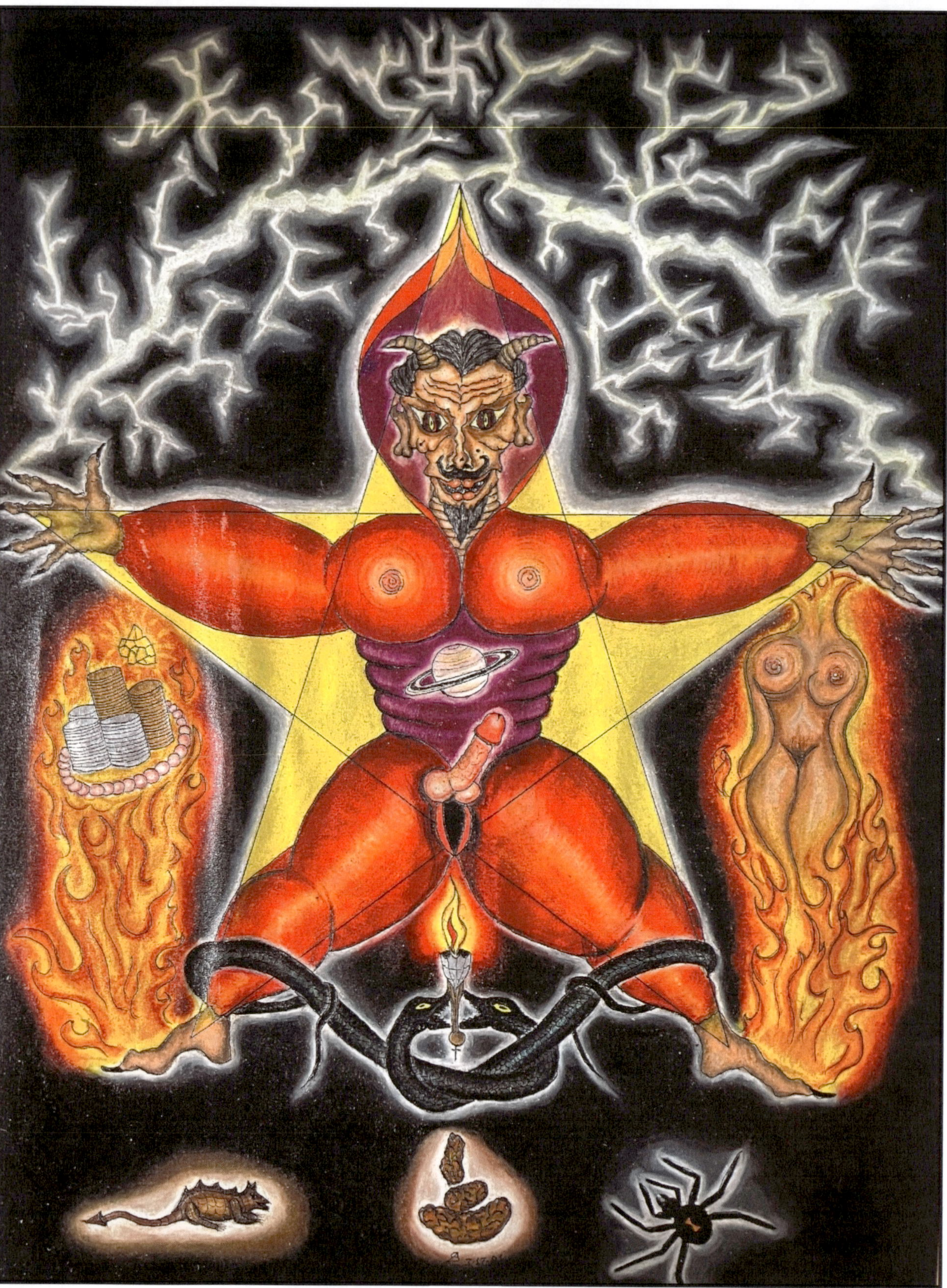

EVIL

Satan is the personification of evil. A philosophical question throughout the ages is whether the devil is a human-made construction of evil or is a dark aspect of the Godhead. Does the omniscient God contain evil, or is it a split-off aspect of the Godhead that has fallen from grace or been banished to create an all-loving deity? Whatever the truth, this image depicts a human-like horned devil with a frightening, disfigured head. It is superimposed on the pentagram, wearing a bloated red suit indicative of ego inflation, narcissism, and self-indulgence. The human correspondence would be the malignant narcissist or psychopath, without conscience, accountability, empathy, or self-awareness, bent on exploitation and domination. The soulless devil is isolated and wants to procure one from the companionship of a human in exchange for promises of material and worldly status, symbolized by the flames emanating money, gold, and greed. It's the devil at the crossroads. Perhaps the soulless devil collects human souls to counter the all-loving God as an act of retribution for being abandoned by the Deity. The voluptuous female figure without a face represents lustful sexuality without conscience or love. Instead of a heart in the center lies Saturn, the planet exemplifying melancholy, isolation, non-feeling, distance, and coldness.

Below, the male and female sexual organs are seen, representing the exploitation of lust. The black poisonous snakes hold the torch under the genitals. Underneath is excrement, a black widow spider, and a dragon-like rat, symbolizing filth and fear. In the uppermost area are lightning bolts, Satan's power, and in the center is a swastika, a reminder of a terrible manifestation of evil that has taken place.

Whether or not evil is archetypal or the imagined darkness of humanity, it creates chaos and destroys order. While easily projected onto other people or groups, for any individual, it requires integration as an aspect of the human shadow, personally and collectively. Evil is not amoral, as with the destruction caused by an earthquake or flood, but is immoral and with a conscious intent.

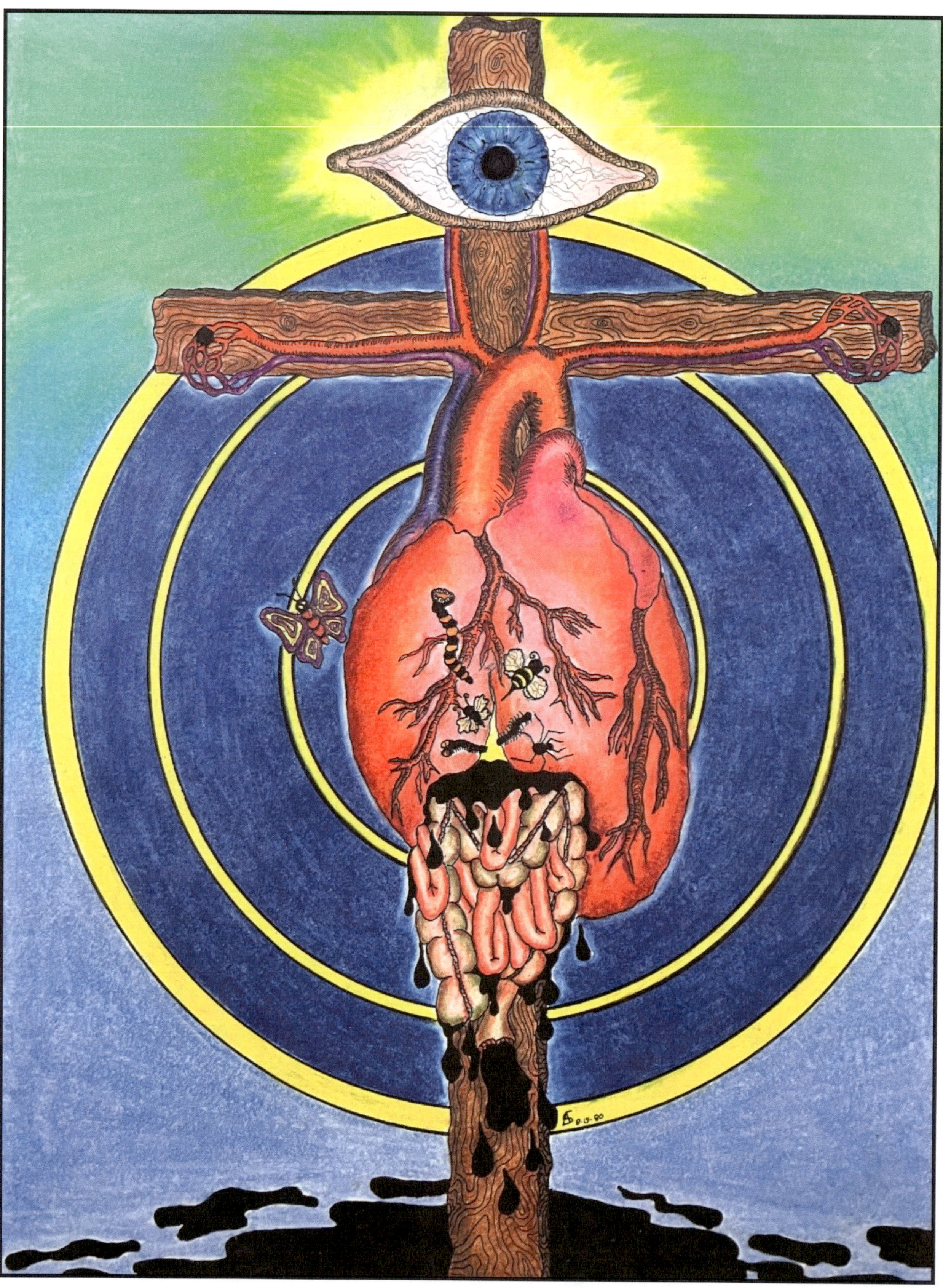

PURGING PSYCHIC TOXICITY

In this image, a heart is pinned to the cross, representative of Christ's crucifixion as well as the pain and sacrifice experienced by human suffering. The cross displays the vertical and horizontal aspects of the tree of life. The tree's base sends its roots downward, and the top ascends to connect with the spiritual realm. The horizontal plane represents the difficult aspects of existence we encounter in present reality and are pinned to in life. The psychological traumas of sadness, loss, anger, and negative emotions clutter the psyche and are often repressed and held within, blocking the flow of psychic energy and preventing progress in life.

When the heart opens, a catharsis of these suppressed emotions of the heart and the gut releases vermin and accumulated psychological poisons. The image symbolizes this toxicity as disembowelment and the purging of dark bile stuck in the psyche. It is when humans are most vulnerable to other people and experiences. For the individual, it is a necessary phase in healing to feel the pain of lancing the boil; it takes courage to do so. Often, more pain occurs before healing, much like having surgery. Yet it is a sign of true strength when confronting this darkness, which otherwise would prevent psychological individuation. Note the butterfly's emergence as the vermin is released, symbolizing the freeing of the suppressed soul. At the top of the image is the ever-present eye of awareness, representing witnessing this event, thus making it conscious and sharing the pain. The purging of psychic toxicity may be accomplished by intensive psychotherapy or shamanic healing practices. The sacred plant medicine ayahuasca is often used for this purging and healing.

A recurrent theme in many of these images is the interplay between the opposites of light and darkness. Suffering in life is inevitable and is a form of slow ego death. Once one surrenders to this death, transformation is possible into a transpersonal bejeweled realm filled with bright light, luminosity, numinosity, and unity. A person becomes one with universal consciousness, sometimes referred to as God. Suffering ends once this purification and transcendence occurs. Death and rebirth are hallmarks experienced figuratively many times during one's lifetime. Time is not linear but circular, like nature's seasons, but soul life is eternal and somehow seeks reincarnation into a physical body, according to certain religious beliefs. Death and rebirth is an archetypal event as noted in the seasons and when a human is initiated into the transpersonal dimension. It is a feature of the healer's journey.

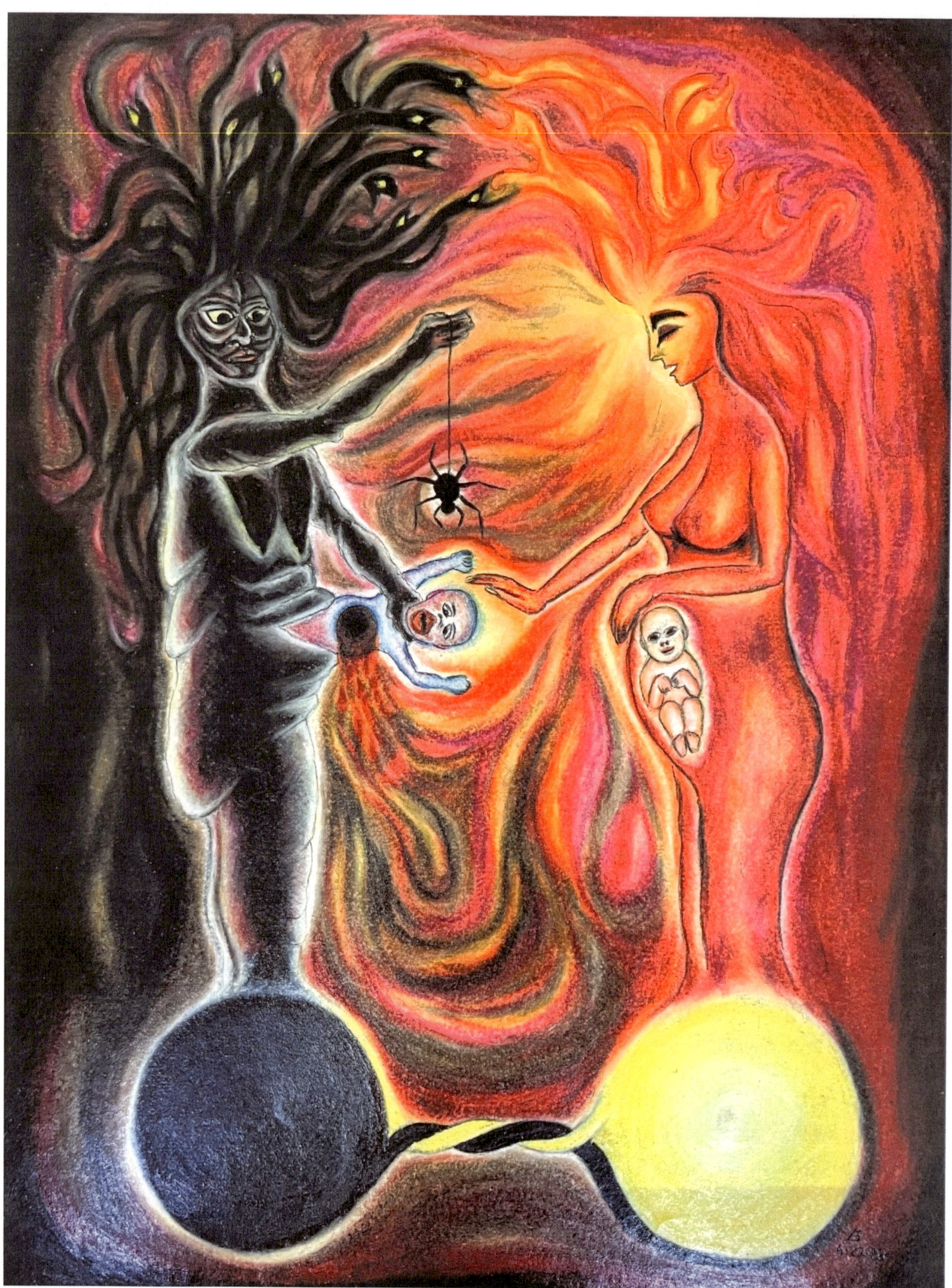

THE WOUNDED AND THE RADIANT CHILD

All archetypes have interconnected positive and negative aspects, ideal and shadow attributes. In this illustration, the good mother is protecting her yet unborn child and holding out her hand in blessing to the terrified child being wrenched out of the womb of the dark mother, Medusa. This traumatic experience leaves a hole and a void in the child's soul. The dangling black spider represents the negative mother and fear.

The good mother provides nourishment, protection, and nurturance to her divine child, providing security and love. The dark mother neglects, abandons, frightens, and traumatizes her newborn. Good and evil are intertwined in the archetypal realm, but there is hope that there may be "good enough" mothering in the personal world to help the child survive, thrive, develop, and live out its radiant essence.

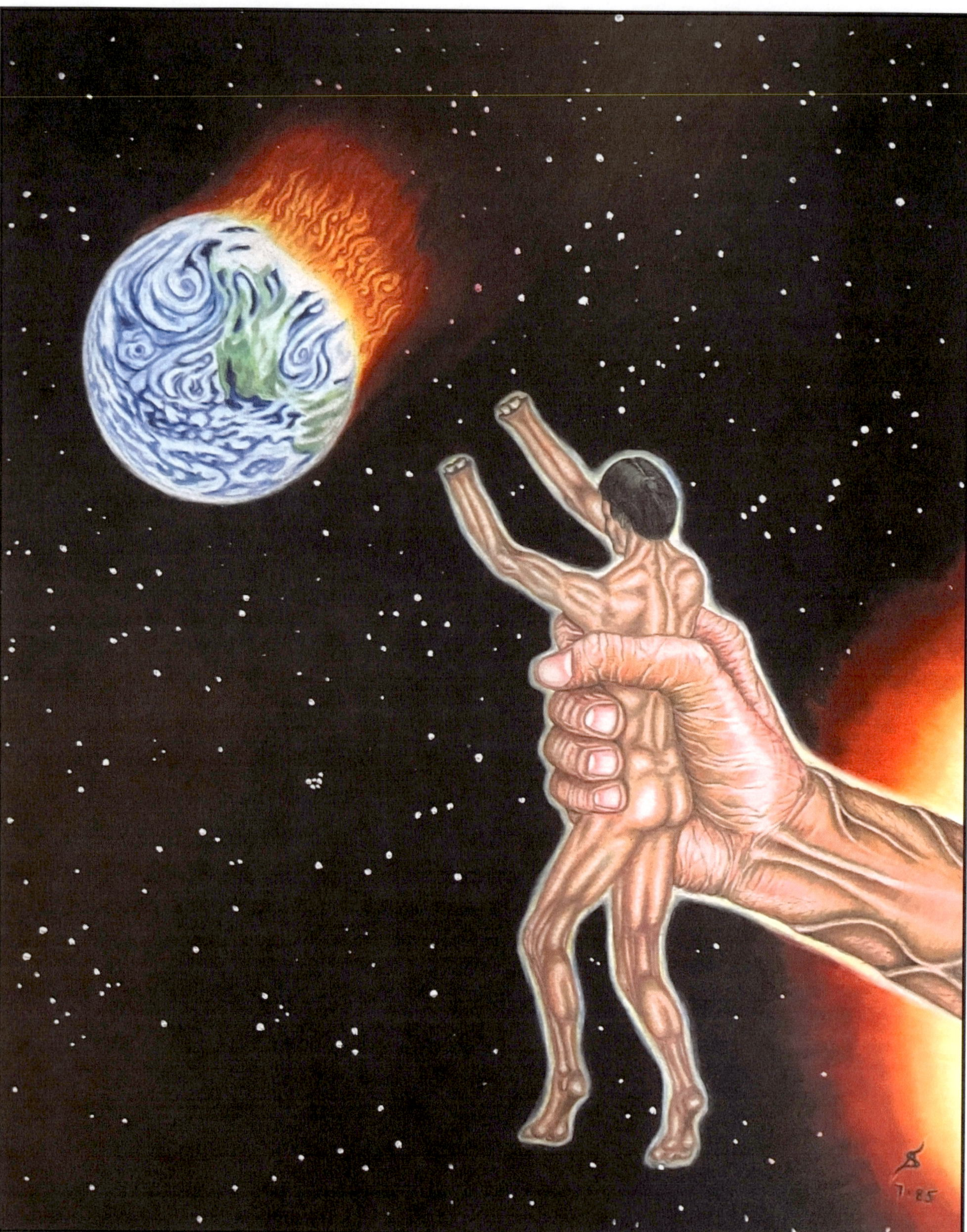

APOCALYPTIC DREAM

This image portrays a human figure who is naked, stripped of his protective clothing, vulnerable, and drifting alone through the stars and the universe. He feels abandoned and is witnessing the apocalypse of the world. Abandonment and death are two main fears that most humans experience during their lifetime. The apocalypse was first described in the Biblical stories of Noah's flood and the Four Horsemen of the Apocalypse from the Book of Revelation. The apocalypse can now be comprehended by climate change, with a world in flames because of rising temperatures or flooding by rising sea levels, severe storms, and environmental degradation. It is also seen in the world with multiple destructive wars and fears of nuclear obliteration. Epidemics, overpopulation challenges, food and proper waste resources, economic instability, grid security, and cyber threats to the internet and communication networks are also present. Artificial intelligence also challenges the future status of humanity as it transitions to a virtual reality and a foreboding of the extinction of all life on earth as we know it.

The man observes this destruction and has lost his hands, symbolizing helplessness. Living with all these fears has severely traumatized the man, and he is now disconnected and separated from a world beyond his grasp. As he observes the earth being destroyed by human folly, his disconnection makes him realize he no longer has any power to do anything about it. The lack of connection and love isolates him from his past life, leading him to feel abandoned and alone, drifting into a dark universe. Although he no longer is of the world, the arm and hand of the Divine has him in a firm grasp. It symbolizes an experience of ego death and a connection with the transpersonal dimension. All he can do is surrender to this fate. The arm emanates from a source of light, representing a divine presence and faith for rebirth and survival.

No wonder our most prominent fears are abandonment and death. Hopefully, his dream is not prophetic.

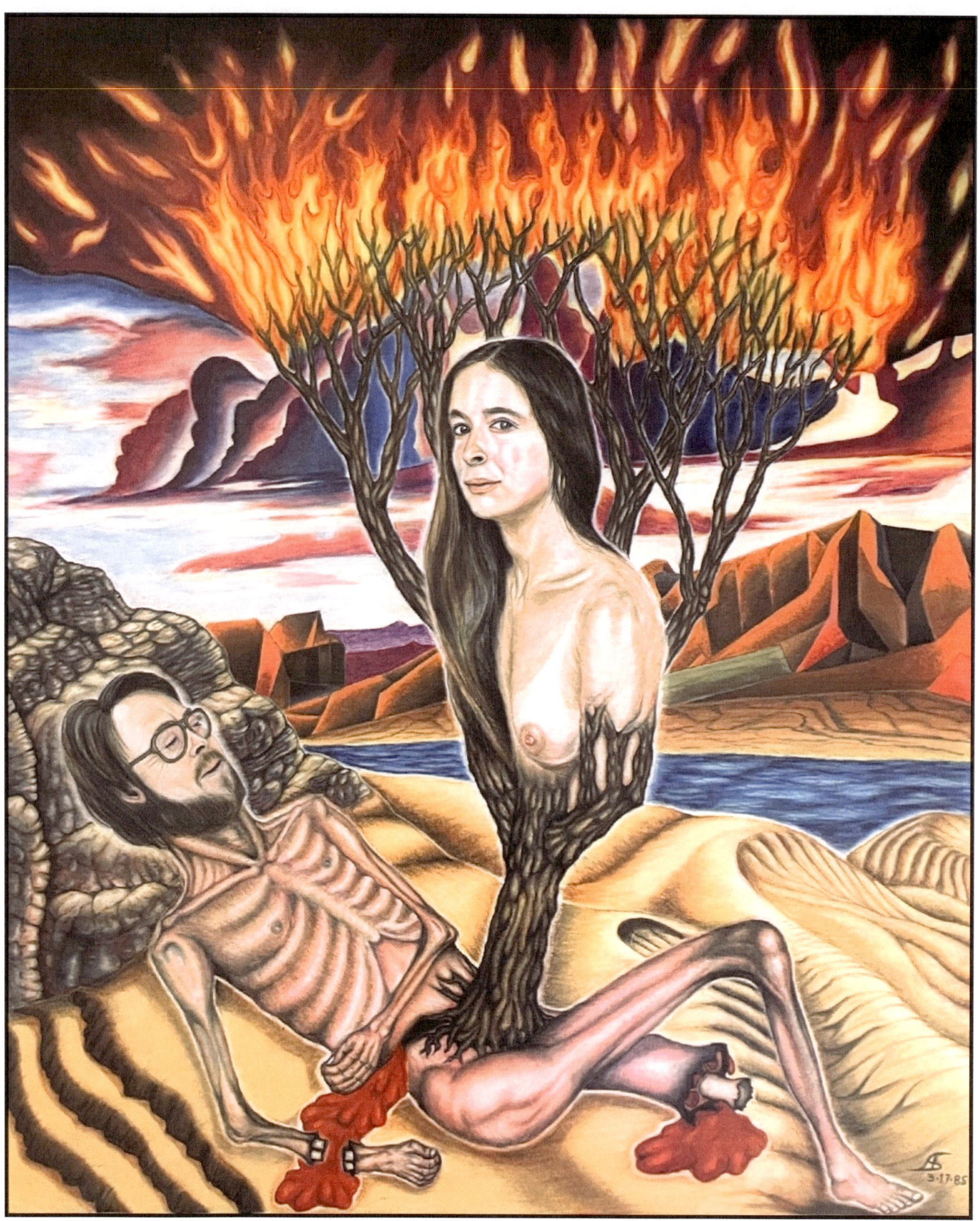

THE WOUNDED HEALER

This image depicts an emaciated, severely wounded, and dismembered man that I drew when I was younger, during a period of depression. With closed eyes, he envisions a beautiful woman within a flaming tree that emerges from his loins. In the background is a barren desert with a flowing stream, representing the movement of life energy. Life or death is in the balance. In his fantasy, she symbolizes the inspirational Muse with the hope that she will redeem him from the land of the dead through her love and compassion. In Jungian psychology, she represents his anima, which in this depressed state can easily be projected onto a woman who becomes attracted to a "wounded bird" man she wants to nurture and nurse.

The danger of projecting the anima onto a real person usually leads to disappointment since the actual woman embodies her own attributes rather than the fantasy and needs of a man. Working through this psychological material is vital to avoid projecting these unreasonable expectations that can never be fulfilled by a real person. It is often a psychodynamic of a destructive love affair or marriage gone wrong.

This image of mortification depicts ego death and an incubation period before rebirth is possible. At times, a crisis is necessary for change to transpire. It is said that "only the wounded healer can heal" by bringing a window of personal insight into a patient's traumatized psyche. "Dismemberment" symbolizes a deconstruction or fragmentation of the psyche. By "remembering" (rememberment) the wound in psychotherapy or with entheogenic journey work, the psyche is reconstructed, leading to healing and retrieval of soul loss. Healing brings back order from chaos.

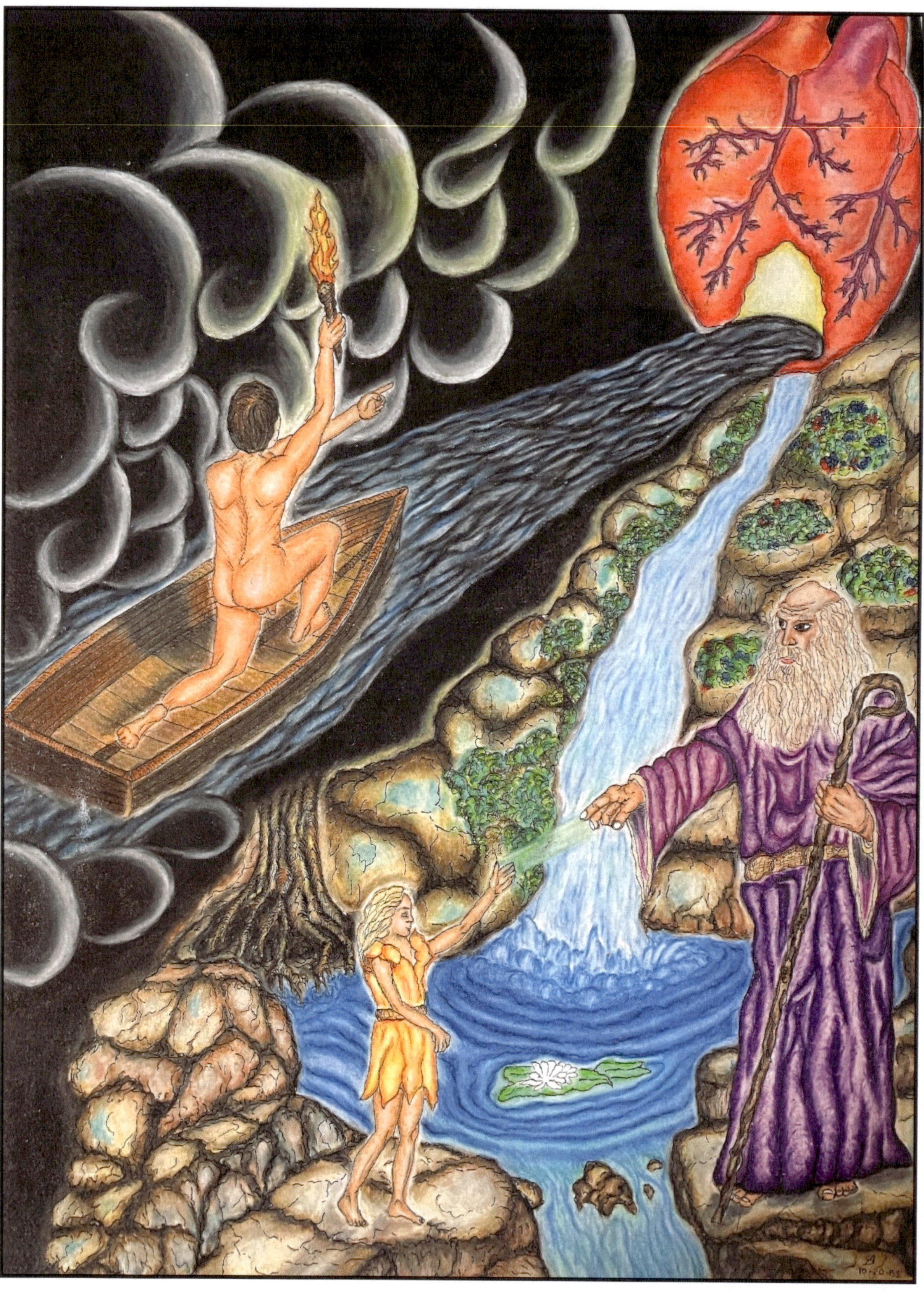

THE DARK NIGHT OF THE SOUL AND HOPE

Experiencing the Dark Night of the Soul, or the Night Sea Journey, can be terrifying. One feels hopeless, abandoned, lost, and depressed, as if approaching death, annihilation, and ablation of all awareness. In this image, a naked, vulnerable man drifts on a black river in a boat without a rudder. When all hope is lost, the man holds up a torch, illuminating his path. Ahead, he sees a beating heart with a door-like opening through which a light blazes, representing the return of hope as his boat enters this lighted threshold.

The scene changes to a flowing waterfall emptying into a pond with a lotus blossom floating in the center. On the right, an old wise man with the staff of authority reaches across the water to a young, orphaned girl who is also reaching out to him. He represents a benevolent father figure to guide and protect her. Energy is transmitted between them as they are both alone and longing for a connection and a bond. She represents new life, hope, and a reinvigorating spirit and soul to the elder. She symbolizes the young female Puella (Latin) archetype. The wise man, the Senex (Latin), is knowledgeable and transmits wisdom to the world. The man may be wise, but he has become old, rigid, and dry and no longer possesses the vitality of youth. Together, a relationship forms, exchanging the spontaneity and energy of youthfulness for the protection and nurturance of a good father. It represents the conjunction (coniunctio) of wisdom with eros but without sexuality. It is the joining of two souls, thought to exist beyond time and space and in an eternal realm, so age differences are irrelevant.

When one survives the encounter with the Dark Night, grace follows, then wisdom and enlightenment.

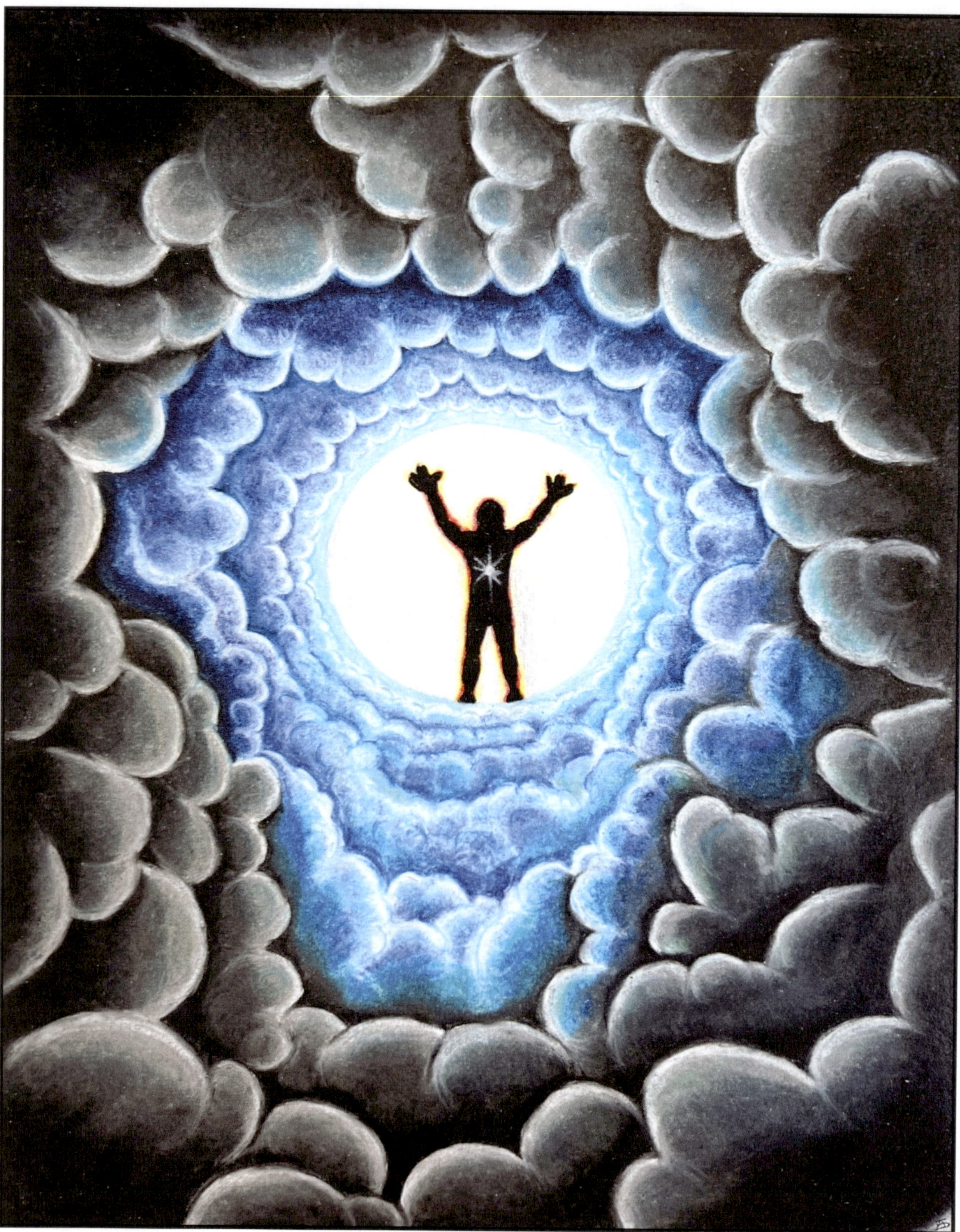

EMERGENCE OF THE ANTHROPOS

Consciousness emerges from unconsciousness and light from darkness. It is the Big Bang within the human psyche. The dark storm clouds open to reveal pure light. The Anthropos, a human-like figure, emerges and raises his hands, creating the Hebrew "Shin" sign, representing faith, hope, and love.

It symbolizes humanity's discovery and praise of the divine essence within – the birth of consciousness and the recognition of love as a universal principle in the cosmos and on the earth. As consciousness evolves over time, it manifests an ever-expanding reality, eventually leading to the awareness of the Creator. In one word, Hallelujah!

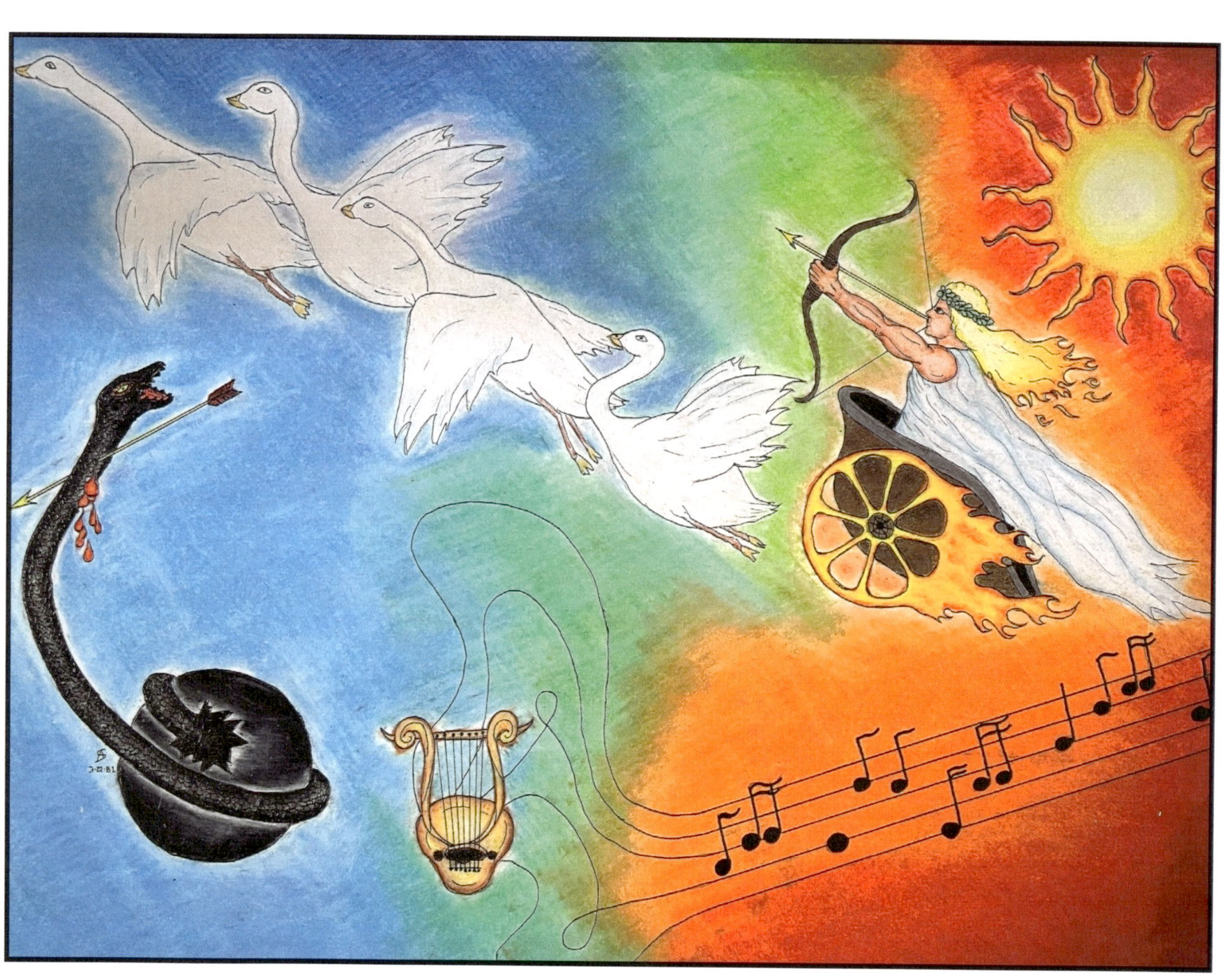

APOLLO — GOD OF LIGHT

feel a strong connection to the Greek god Apollo. He was the son of Zeus and Leto and the twin brother of Artemis. Apollo was known as the god of music, archery, prophecy, and healing. He embodied the traits of strength, insight, clarity, and loftiness of spirit. He is known for bringing order from chaos and was a god of light and the sun. His instruments were the bow and arrow and the seven-stringed lyre. He brings wisdom and truth from the instinctual realm to the conscious world.

In Greek mythology, he slays the python at Delphi with his bow, which had tried to prevent his birth and kill his mother. He also gave birth to the great physician Asklepios. He also represents the function of withdrawal, as he periodically left for the Nordic realm, the land of the Hyperboreans, in the autumn and returned in the mild weather of Spring, drawn by swans in his golden chariot. He required periodic isolation to rejuvenate himself from the world of activity. It is reminiscent of Persephone's cyclical return in the Spring from the underworld, as she also represents the changing seasons.

The symbols of the bow and lyre were intertwined in ancient times. The archer's bow produces musical tones and is able to hit the mark with a song. Apollo was also depicted with long blond hair, indicating his connection to youth and the sun. He was often seen as the initiator of youth to adulthood.

Let us invoke this god from the Hymn to Apollo by Callimachus.

"...not unto everyone doth Apollo appear, but unto him (her) that is good. Who hath seen Apollo, he (she) is great...Golden is the tunic of Apollo and golden his mantle, his lyre, and his bow and his quiver..."

As a healer, musician, and artist, Apollo is my mentor from Greek mythology who represents clarity of thinking, light, and hope; therefore, I honor him in this image.

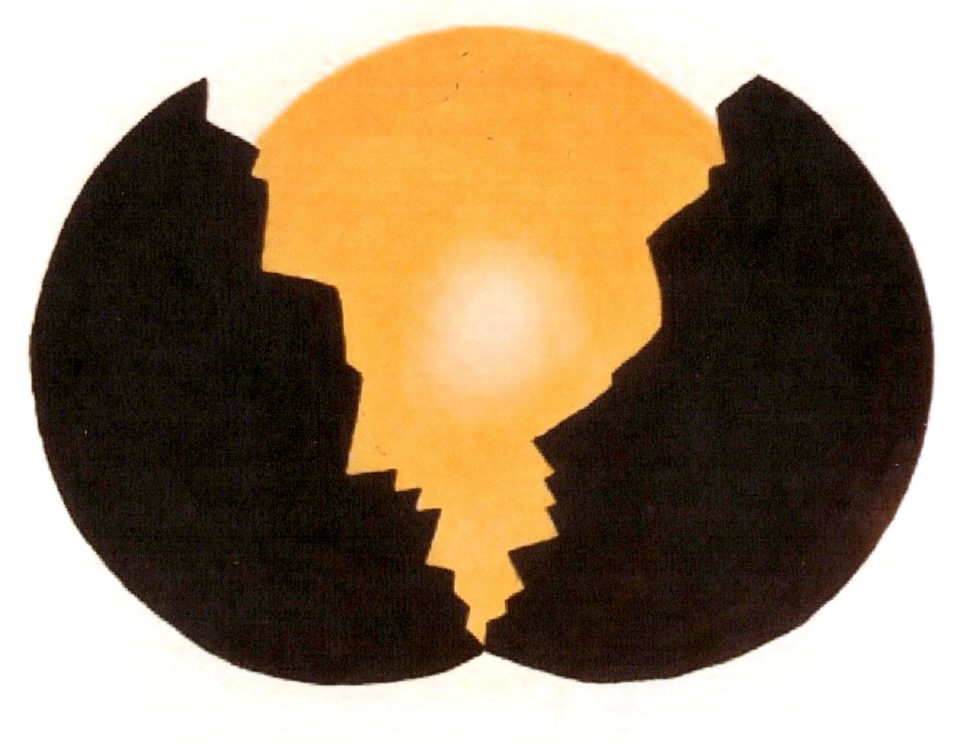

LET THERE BE LIGHT

The universe as we know it came into existence from darkness by a massive explosion called the Big Bang or Big Inflation, from an infinitely small point of light and boundless energy known as the singularity. This light energy expanded and created the galaxies, stars, and planets. Similarly, human consciousness evolved from this infinite and eternal unity into duality and differentiated into space and time, light and dark, and good and evil. Human awareness participates in evolving reality as we perceive it. The observer affects the outcome according to quantum theory, thus creating their own reality. Between this brilliant light and opaque darkness lies a gentle glow that resembles twilight, candlelight, or the partial shadow seen in eclipses, known as the penumbra. In this subtle zone, the soul is encountered.

According to the Kabbalah, before the singularity, the unseen and unknown God, known as the En Sof, emerged into manifestation symbolized by the ten branches of the Sephiroth, representing various traits of the human experience. Analogously, in the Biblical story of Adam and Eve, they are banished from the Garden of Eden, paradise, once they eat the sacred apple (perhaps a sacred mushroom) that made them conscious, which is the original sin that differentiated human awareness from animals. Leaving the unity of unconsciousness, they now experience the duality and sufferings of life beyond this naïve and childlike state called paradise but yearn for the eternal return to this paradisal home, but this time consciously.

The second image depicts the dual emergence of good and evil, with the Godhead image taking on a human-like form but remaining attached to a malevolent figure.

Consciousness erupts from unconsciousness and then creates reality as we know it.

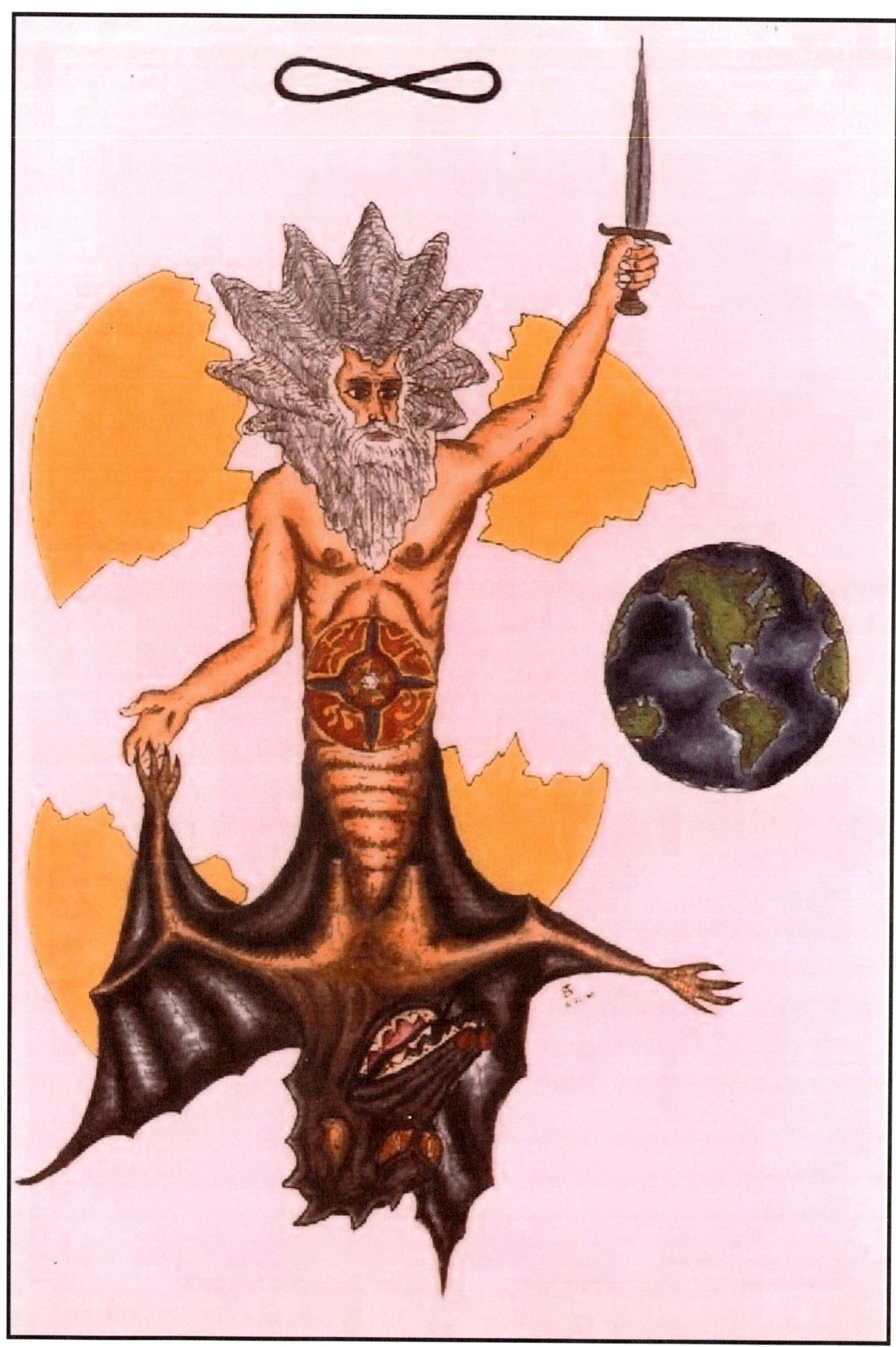

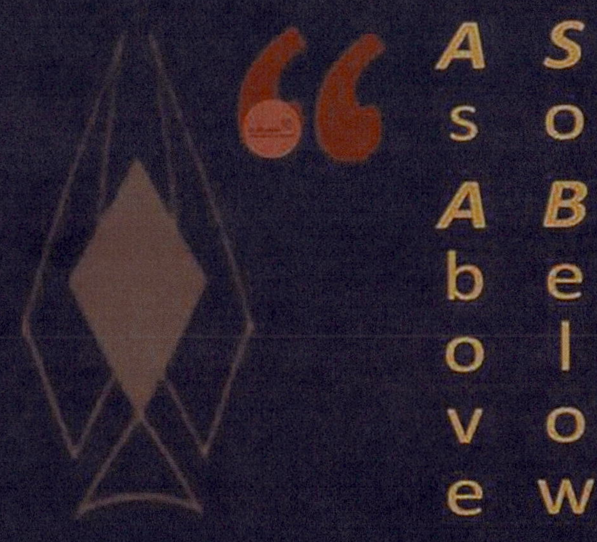

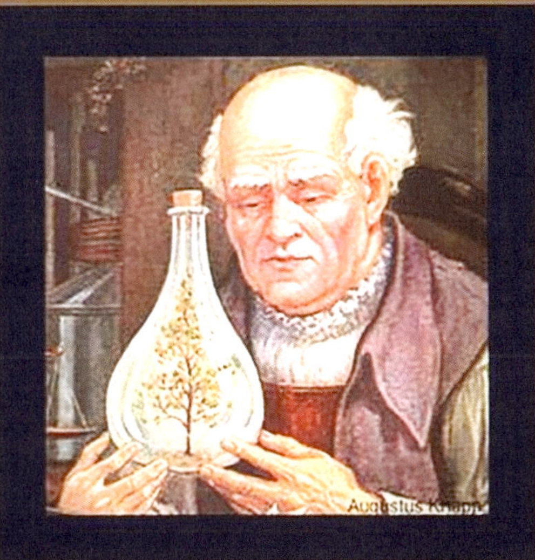

/ The universities do not teach all things... so a doctor must seek out old wives, gypsies, sorcerers, wandering tribes, old robbers, and such outlaws and take lessons from them. A doctor must be a traveler... Knowledge is experience. /

- Paracelsus

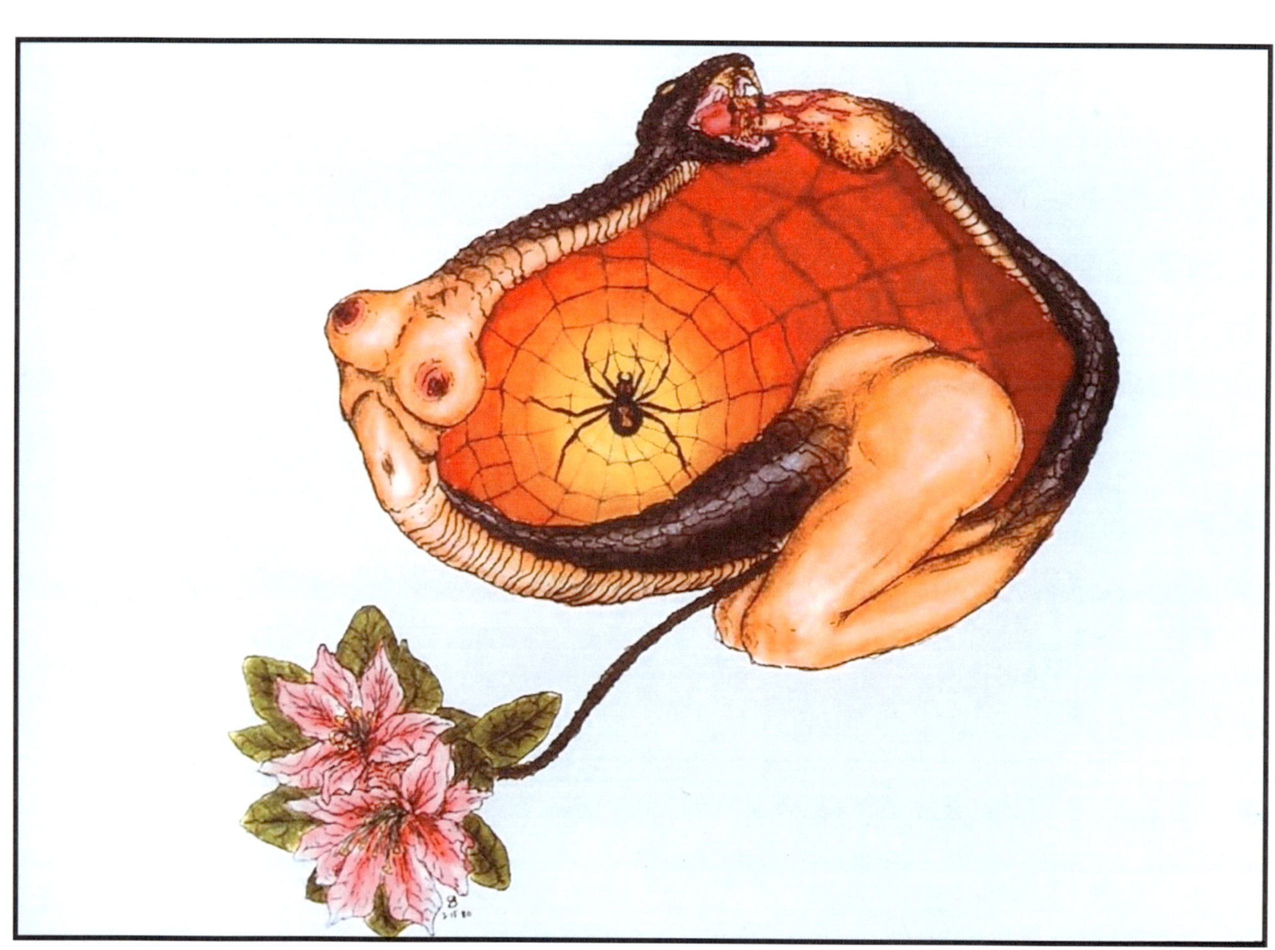

OUROBOROS

Although this illustration first borders on bizarre sexual imagery, it is a symbol known as the ouroboros (or uroboros), which appears in ancient Egyptian, Greek, Gnostic, and alchemical imagery. It is a circular figure of a serpent eating its tail. It symbolizes the cyclic renewal of life, death, and rebirth, a symbol of fertility and eternity, in which the mouth of the snake represents the female yoni and the tail, the male phallus.

Archetypally, it symbolizes the Great Mother in both her positive and negative aspects. In this image, the fertility aspect is seen as the blooming flower emanating from the genital region. In her negative aspect, the black widow spider looms at the center of the picture. The mouth of the serpent is consuming its tail in an act of self-copulation. The exaggerated breasts and buttocks, the erect male member, and the black serpent exemplify the dark, incestual aspect of self-absorption and narcissism, in which the mother does not allow separation and differentiation of the male or son. She thus depotentiates his independent masculinity and obliges him to her service. Psychologically, the son is not allowed to separate from childhood needs, thus fostering dependency; he is stunted in his individuation. He is consumed and tied to the mother complex, never fulfilling his destiny in relationships or work. The Grimm's fairy tale Rapunzel mirrors this dynamic for a female when the sorceress-mother locks her daughter in a tower and tries to prevent her from living an independent life.

I drew this image after learning about the ouroboros during my Jungian studies. This symbol can also represent the pre-ego "dawn state," the undifferentiated child called the prima materia by the ancient alchemists, depicting the unconscious state of a human. It also can represent a feedback loop when duality becomes a unity (circle), thus swallowing and integrating the shadow side of the psyche and bringing the individual wholeness and completion. Symbols can often represent different interpretations depending on the context. The ouroboros is an archetypal symbol in alchemical iconography, as noted in the additional images.

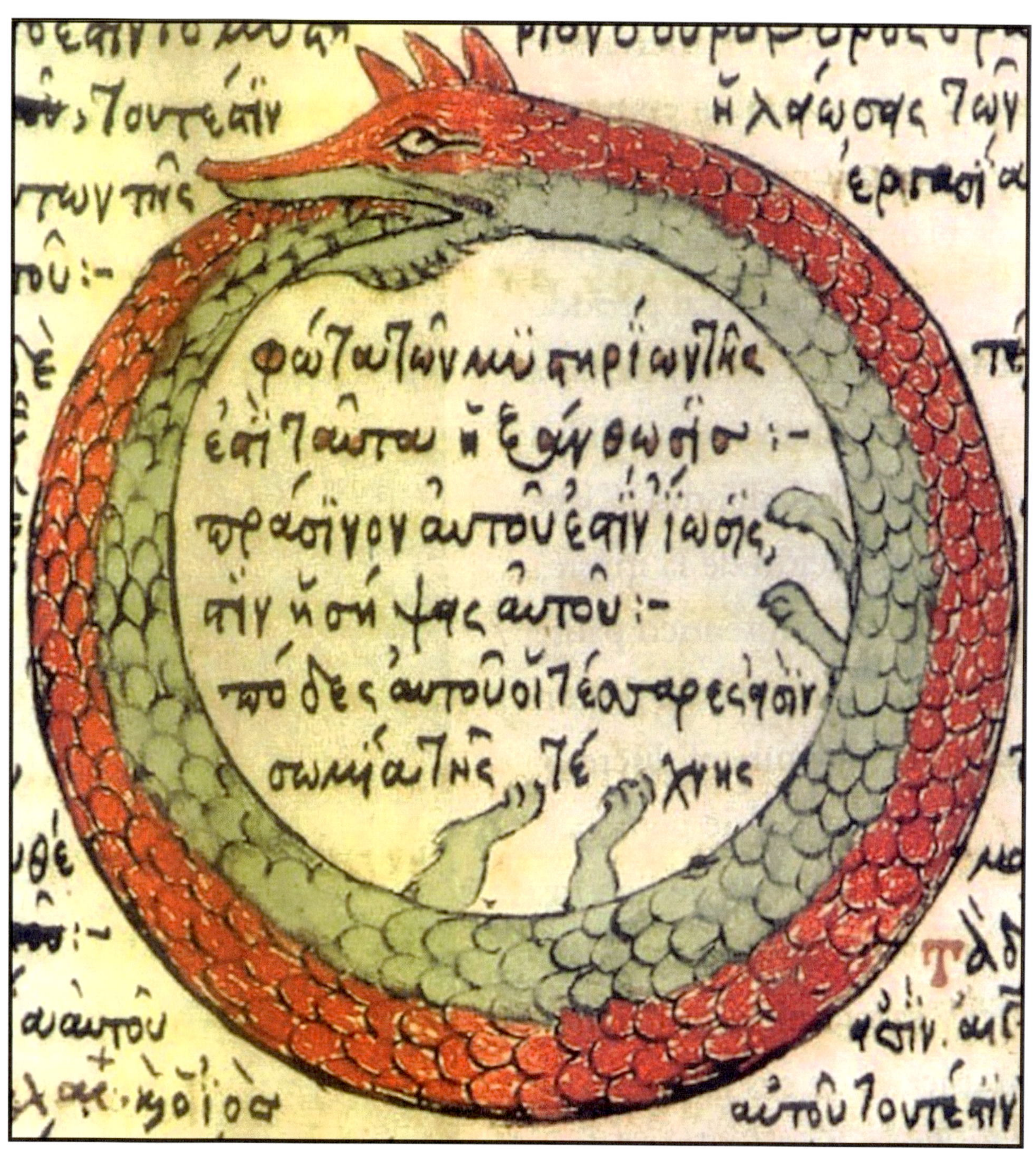
φῶ το τῶν καὶ σωτηρίων τῆς
ἐπὶ ταῦτα ἢ ἐν θωσίσ :-
θρασύτγον αὐτοῦ ἐστιν ἰωσῆς,
τὴν ἡ σήψας αὐτοῦ :-
τῶ δὲς αὐτοῦ οἱ τέσταρες θοὶ
σωμία τῆς τε χης

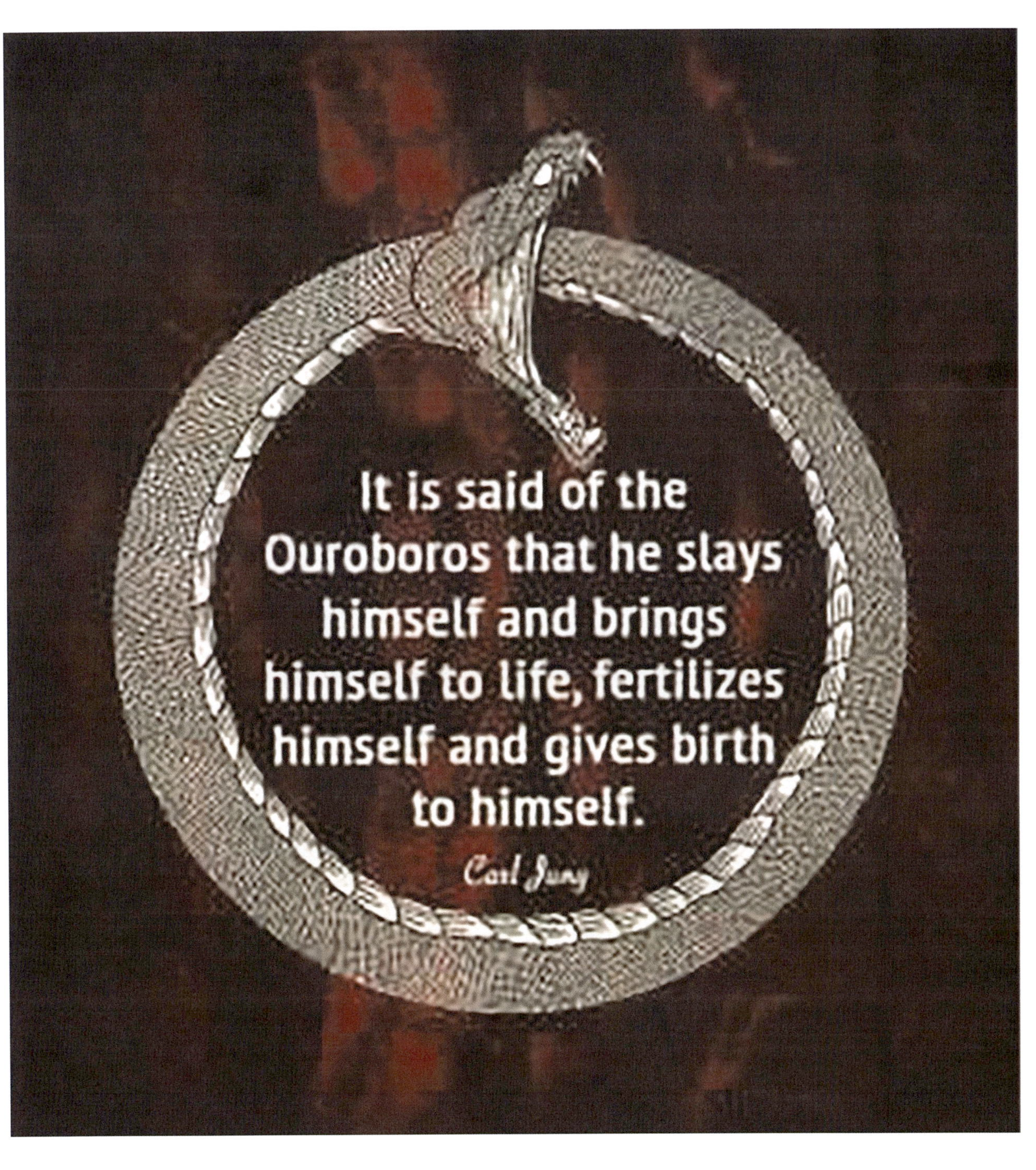
It is said of the
Ouroboros that he slays
himself and brings
himself to life, fertilizes
himself and gives birth
to himself.
Carl Jung

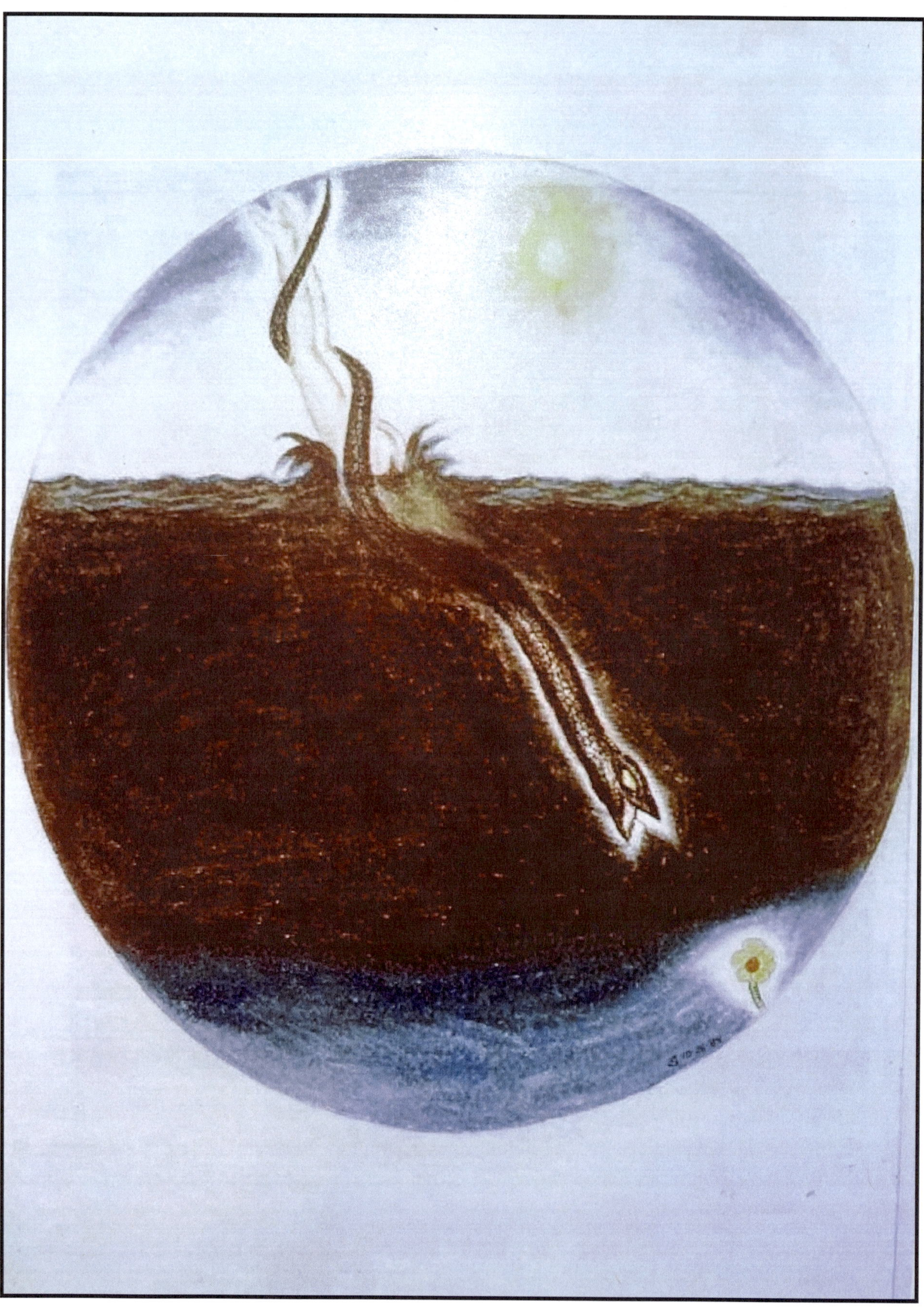

DESCENT TO THE GOLDEN FLOWER

The image portrays a serpent coiling around a human figure, descending into the realm of the unconscious. The journey is being led by our instinctual nature. In daily life, most people do not feel the need to explore the inner world unless they experience psychological trauma or the instinct or intuition to search deeper into their psyche. However, as we age, we may find that the external world fails to offer solutions to our conundrums or offer meaning to our lives. For those who remain curious, a dive into the darkness of the unconscious realm becomes necessary to uncover the hidden aspects of the psyche. By exploring deep enough, one may encounter the greater, transpersonal Self, full of profound mysteries. In these depths, the golden flower of life and light can be rediscovered, leading to a renewed sense of being.

This concept is illustrated in the ancient Taoist text, "The Secret of the Golden Flower: A Chinese Book of Life" by Richard Wilhelm, with commentary by C.G. Jung. This text combines Eastern wisdom with Western thought.

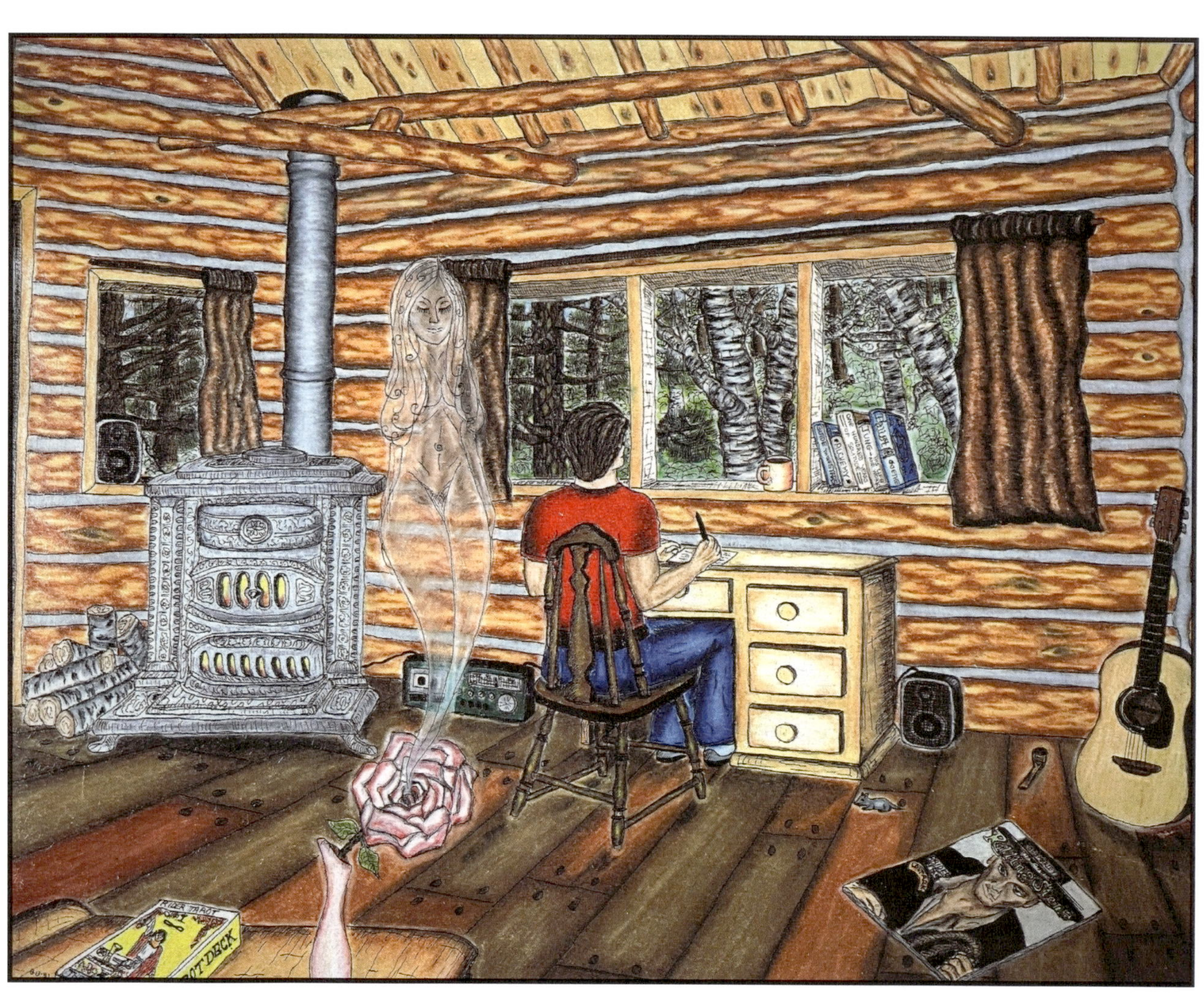

THE INTROVERT

This image is of me many years ago, writing in my journal in a tiny cabin built by my father-in-law, Robert Tipton, in a forest in rural Maine. It was a time when my wife, Judy, and I left Los Angeles and closed my psychiatric practice in West L.A. after my mother died. We grew disillusioned with fast-paced city life and eventually moved and settled in the North County of San Diego. After years of constant education, training, and working, I needed a break from it all before settling down and resuming work as a psychiatrist.

Every day, I would make the short hike up a hill to the cabin, where I could be alone, writing, doing artwork, playing my guitar, reading, and listening to music. In the evening, I would head back to the house to be with my family and in-laws, Bob and Sunny. It was a wonderful time to be with family, explore local lakes, and rejuvenate my spirit.

I found my alone time in the cabin to be productive, and it helped me reconnect with my introverted side. Introversion is when one draws psychic energy from one's inner life in solitude, whereas extroversion is when one derives meaning and sense of self from the outer world. We all are on a spectrum between these two concepts. For the extreme introvert, the outside world can be daunting and sometimes threatening to one's identity. Fortunately, I always compensated for my introverted nature through my relationships with colleagues, friends, patients, and family. Artwork, reading, and writing require focus while alone, which I enjoy. My practice of doing dreamwork, Jungian analysis, and psychedelic and shamanic exploration reinforced these inner values.

In this scene, I illustrate all the above by sitting at a desk where I write in a journal and draw. The forest outside surrounds the cabin, and a few books with titles are on the windowsill, reflecting my current interests. Behind me appears a translucent Muse who inspires my efforts. On the floor, a friendly mouse keeps me company. A guitar, the recent edition of Rolling Stone magazine, a Tarot deck, a portable stereo for music, and the warmth of the wood-burning stove are keeping me content. This experience promoted my mindfulness of an ecstatic state of introversion, which continued throughout my life.

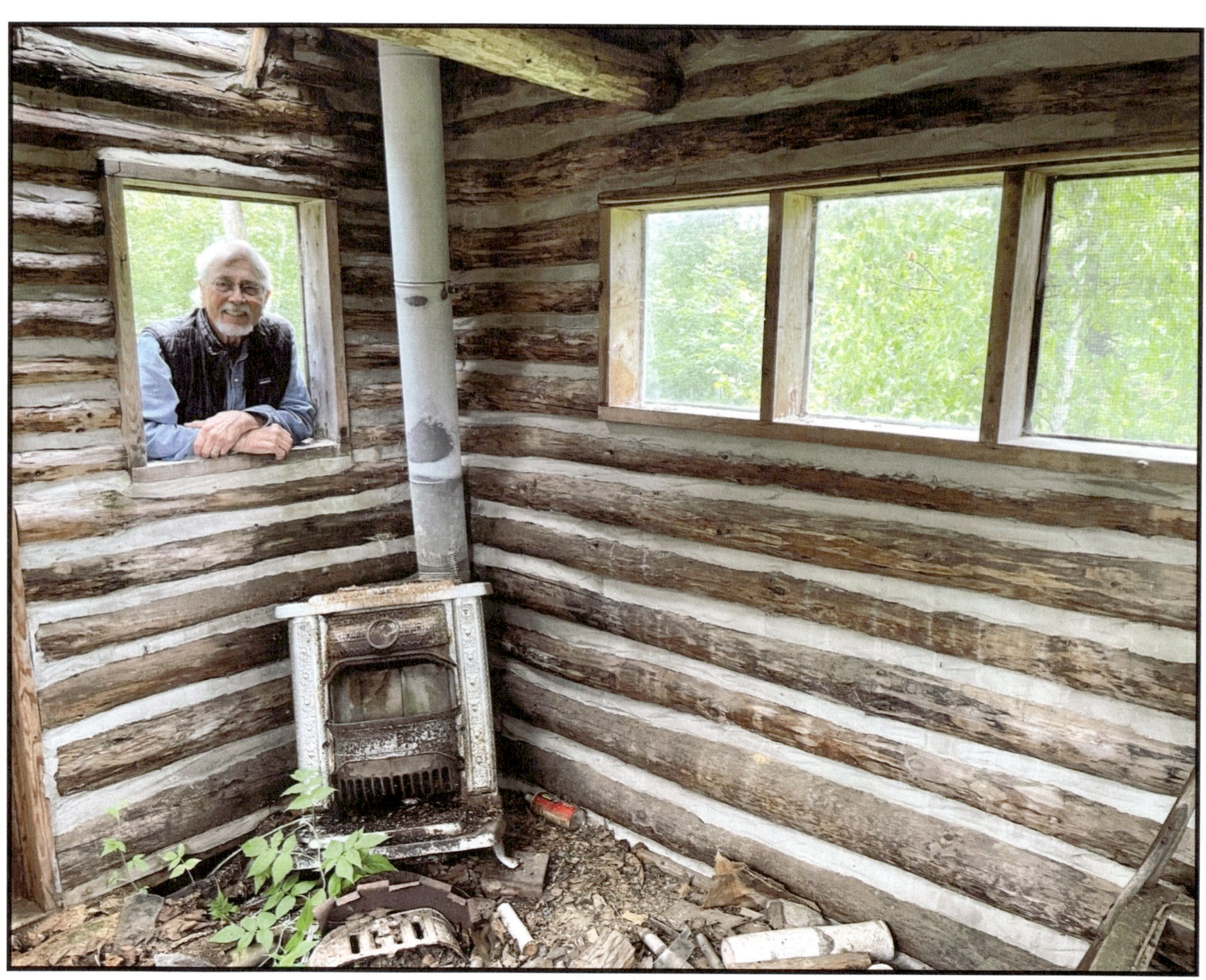

Re-visiting the old, abandoned cabin forty years later, now dilapidated.

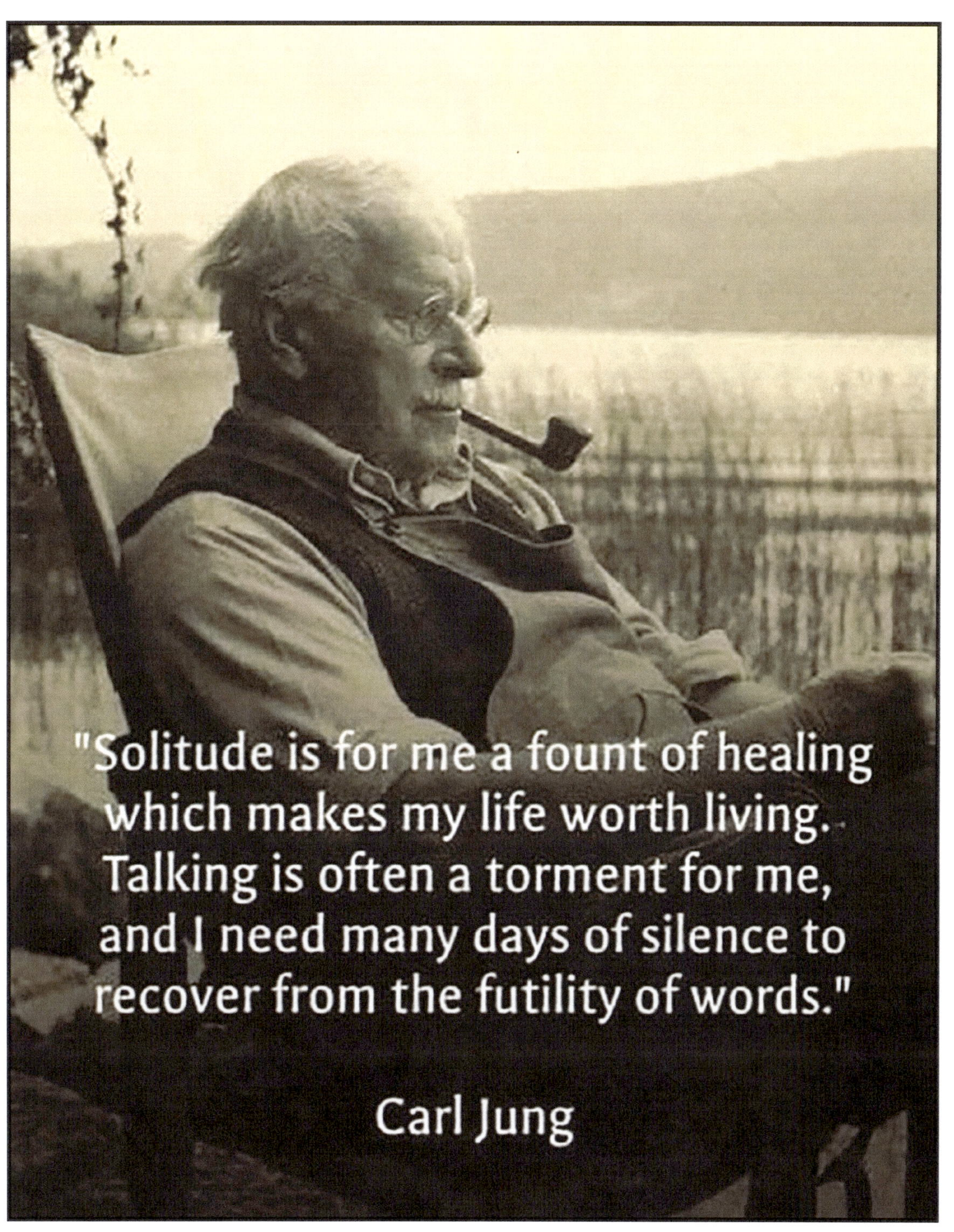
"Solitude is for me a fount of healing
which makes my life worth living.
Talking is often a torment for me,
and I need many days of silence to
recover from the futility of words."

Carl Jung

Additional Older Art

(expanded edition)

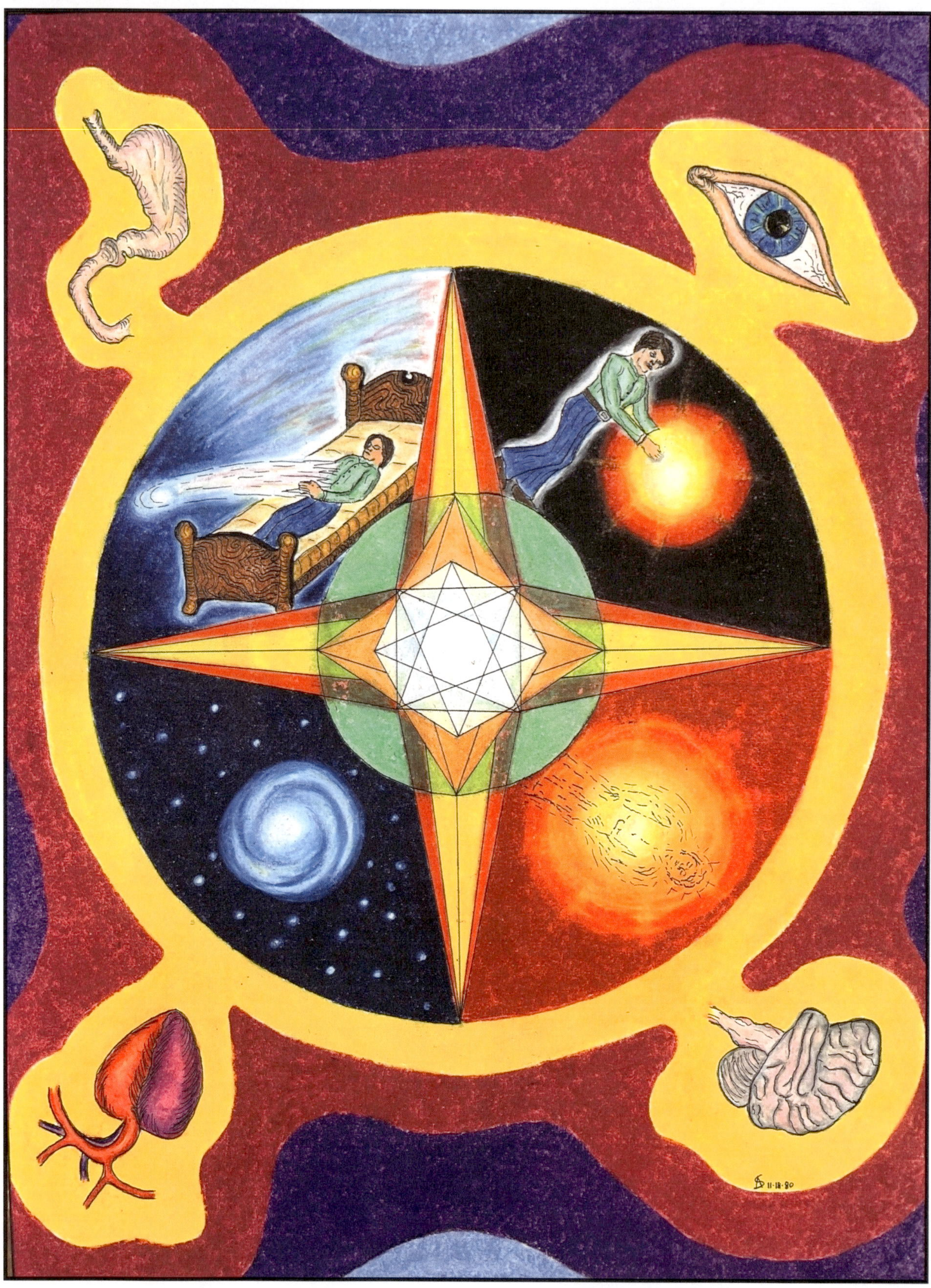

THE FOURFOLD WAY OF TRANSFORMATION

C. G. Jung articulated that mandalas were expressions of the inner Self, and encouraged his patients to draw them, particularly during times of stress or chaos, as a way to regain balance and clarity. In Jungian symbolism, the circle represents the cosmic whole, while the four quadrants reflect the realities of existence. At the center lies the quintessence, depicted by an incorruptible diamond symbolizing the core of being.

A four-pointed star divides the mandala into four sections, illustrating the stages of the transformation process. In the upper right section, the ego-identity first encounters the divine light energy, initiating the journey of transformation. Moving clockwise, the ego dissolves into the light, merging and identifying with the transpersonal Self. In the lower left quadrant, the individual experiences pure cosmic energy, deepening the connection to universal forces. Moving to the upper left, the dreamer must disengage from the cosmic realm and return to human life, now aware of a higher dimension of consciousness. Remaining identified with this state leads to ego inflation and psychopathology.

Surrounding the edges of the mandala, four anatomical images represent essential aspects of the human experience. The all-seeing eye signifies heightened awareness, witnessing the process of transformation. The brain embodies intelligence and reason (logos); the heart reveals the emotions and love (eros); and the stomach, signifying the Chi power center, or instinctual gut knowledge (intuition) that absorbs and integrates the experiences of living.

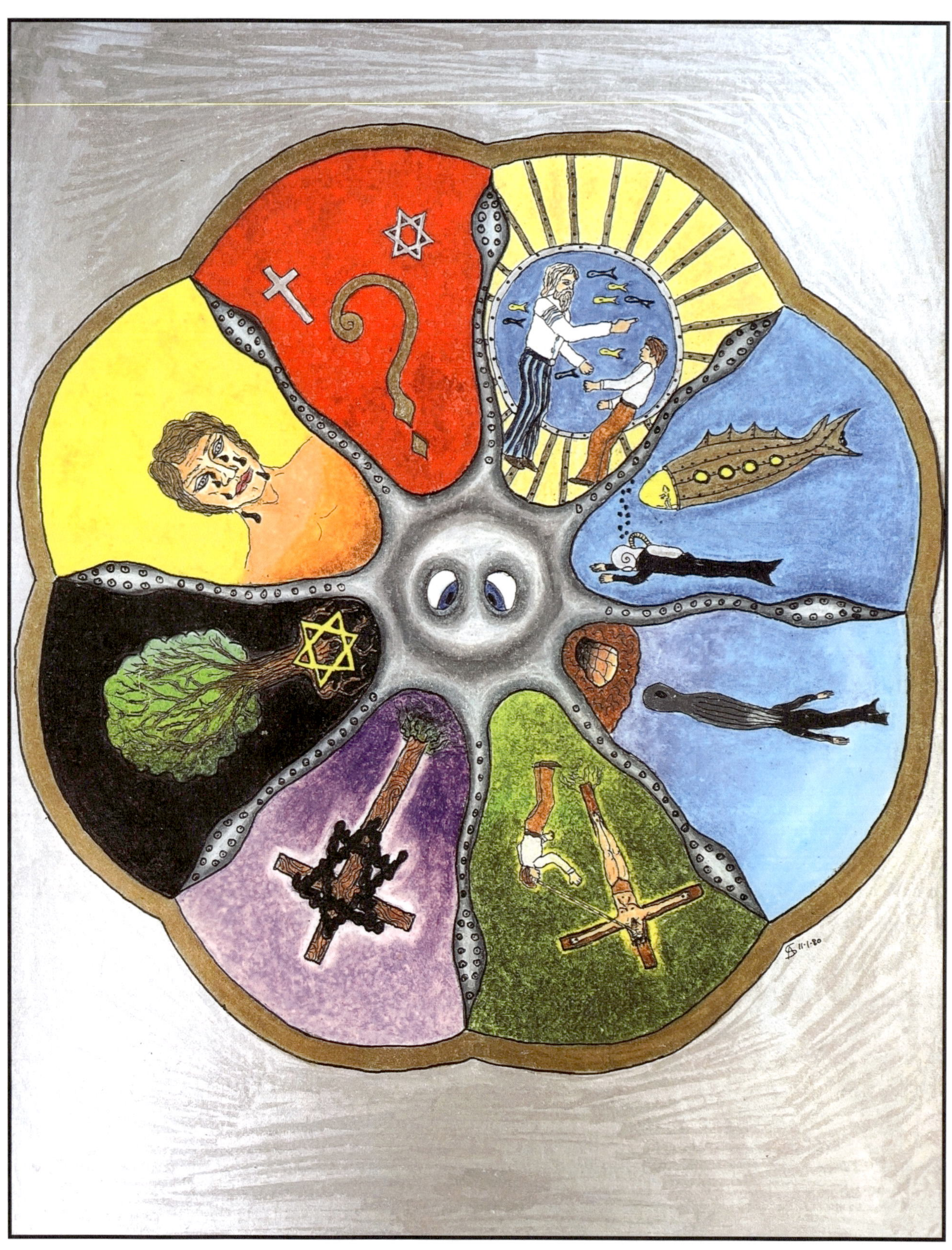

THE CONFLICT OF SPIRITUAL IDENTITY

During a period of confusion regarding my spiritual identity, I created this mandala. Having already distanced myself from the dogma of Judaism, I found myself drawn to further spiritual exploration. While I continued to identify with the Jewish culture, its spiritual aspects felt abstract and remote. At the same time, my dreams and visions began to feature incarnations of the divine, imagery more commonly associated with the Christian experience of the Christ within. Reconciling these conflicting influences proved challenging.

The mandala's central image is an octopus, its eight arms encapsulating scenes from my spiritual journey. In the upper right, I am in a submarine guided by a Captain Nemo figure, symbolizing my need to go out to explore the depths of the undersea, or the unconscious realm. Moving clockwise, I am seized by an octopus and pulled into a cavern, where I witness a crucifixion scene, the divine becoming human, enabling a personal relationship with the sacred.

Next, I see a tarnished Star of David pinned to a cross symbolizing the abstract concept of Yahweh, which never fully integrated into my psyche. Continuing clockwise, the Sacred Tree of Life appears, with its roots entwined with my Jewish identity. The conflict brings me sadness, as I am a Jew who also believes that the incarnation of the divinity marks a transformational step from the ego to the deeper Self, in line with Jungian symbolism. After all, Jesus was Jewish.

Ultimately, the question remains: How can I integrate these two opposing aspects of my psyche? The mandala represents a visual meditation on this unresolved tension, a search for wholeness amid spiritual complexity.

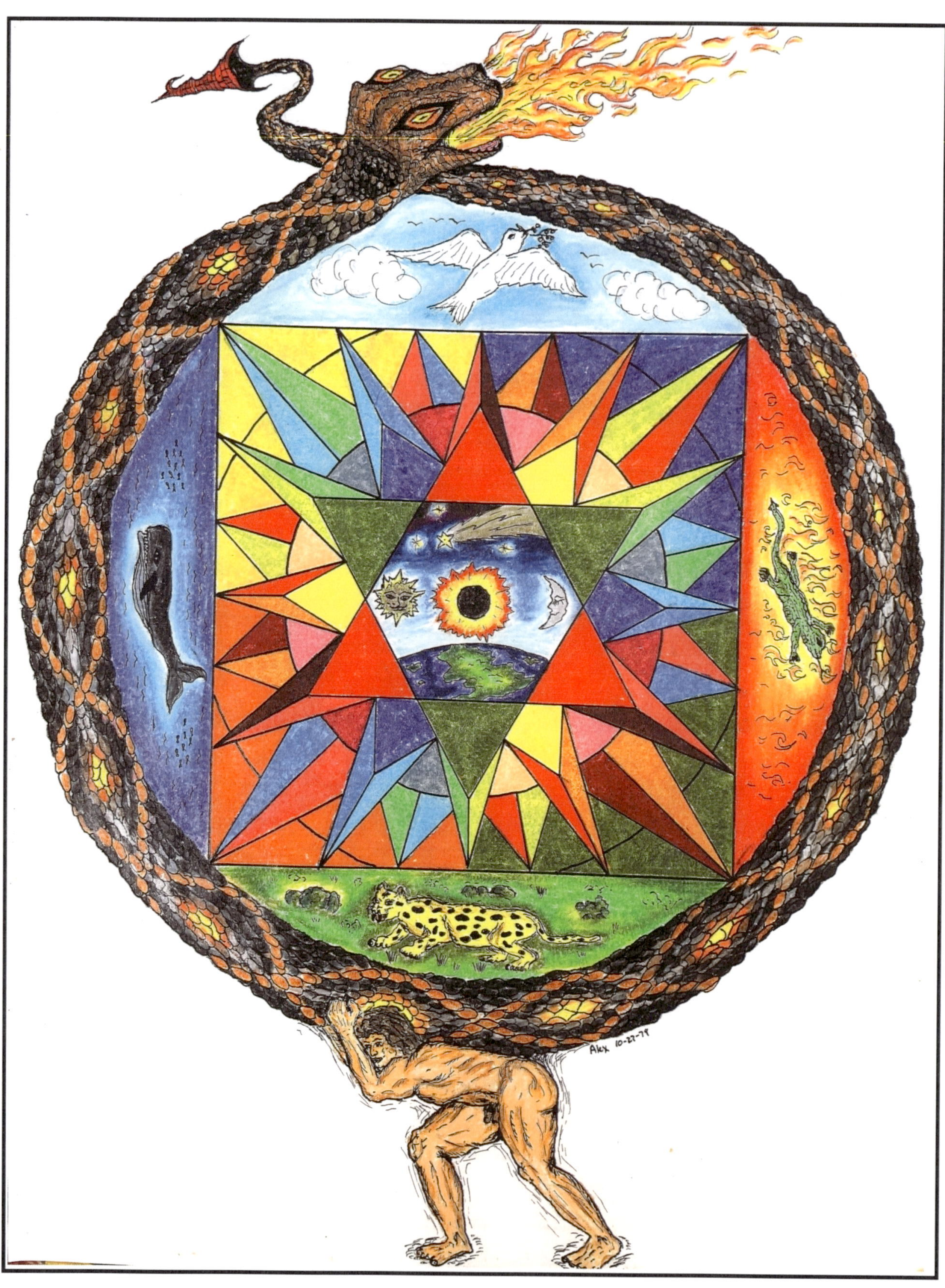

Alex 10-27-79

CARRYING THE WEIGHT
OF THE WORLD

A mandala image of a quadrated circle displays a serpent spewing fire, symbolizing the forces of instinct and transformation. Surrounding the serpent are images of the four elements - Earth, Air, Fire, and Water, representing facets of existence. In the center of the square is the Earth, an eclipse of the sun, and cosmic imagery. The six-pointed star (the Star of David) honors my Jewish heritage. As depicted, I am carrying the burdens of existence as my soul embodies the complexity of life. This early art was from 1979 and was inspired by my Jungian studies and the idea that mandalas symbolize and activate the deeper Self.

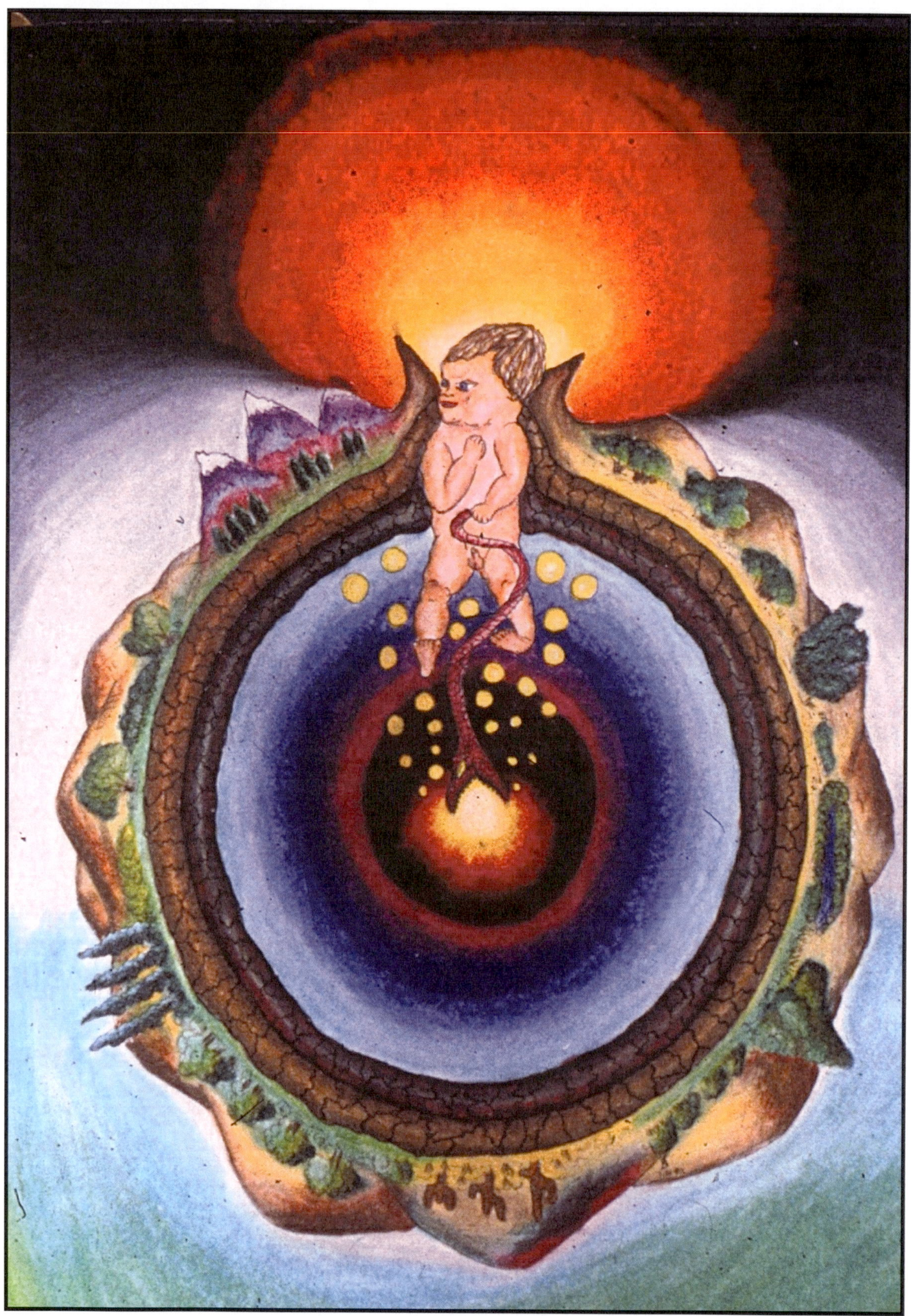

BIRTH

created this image in early 1979 to commemorate the experience of witnessing the birth of my first son in 1978. I was already steeped in mandala imagery, so I envisioned him being born from the Earth's womb to the glory of first light. This piece reflects the primitive style of my early self-taught art, as I learned to transform my unconscious into consciousness through imagery.

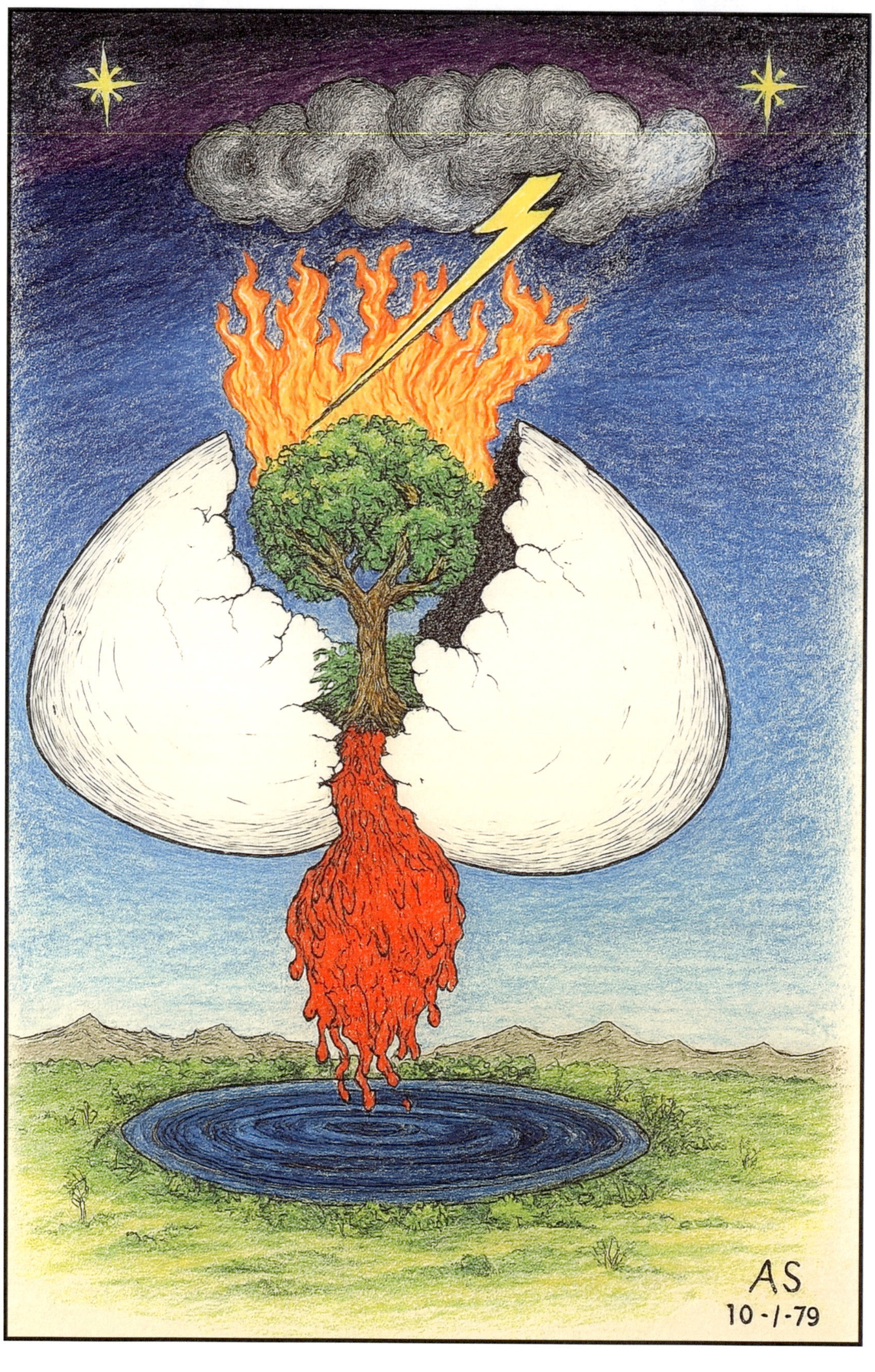
AS
10-1-79

THE COSMIC EGG – THE BEGINNING OF AWARENESS

This artwork is one of my earliest explorations with colored pencils. It symbolizes the beginning of consciousness: the Cosmic Egg, a symbol of origin, cracks open, releasing the contents of the unconscious with the emergence of a burning tree, representing the energy of transformation. The roots express blood and a heart flowing into a calm pool of water, signifying the merging of emotion and life into the world.

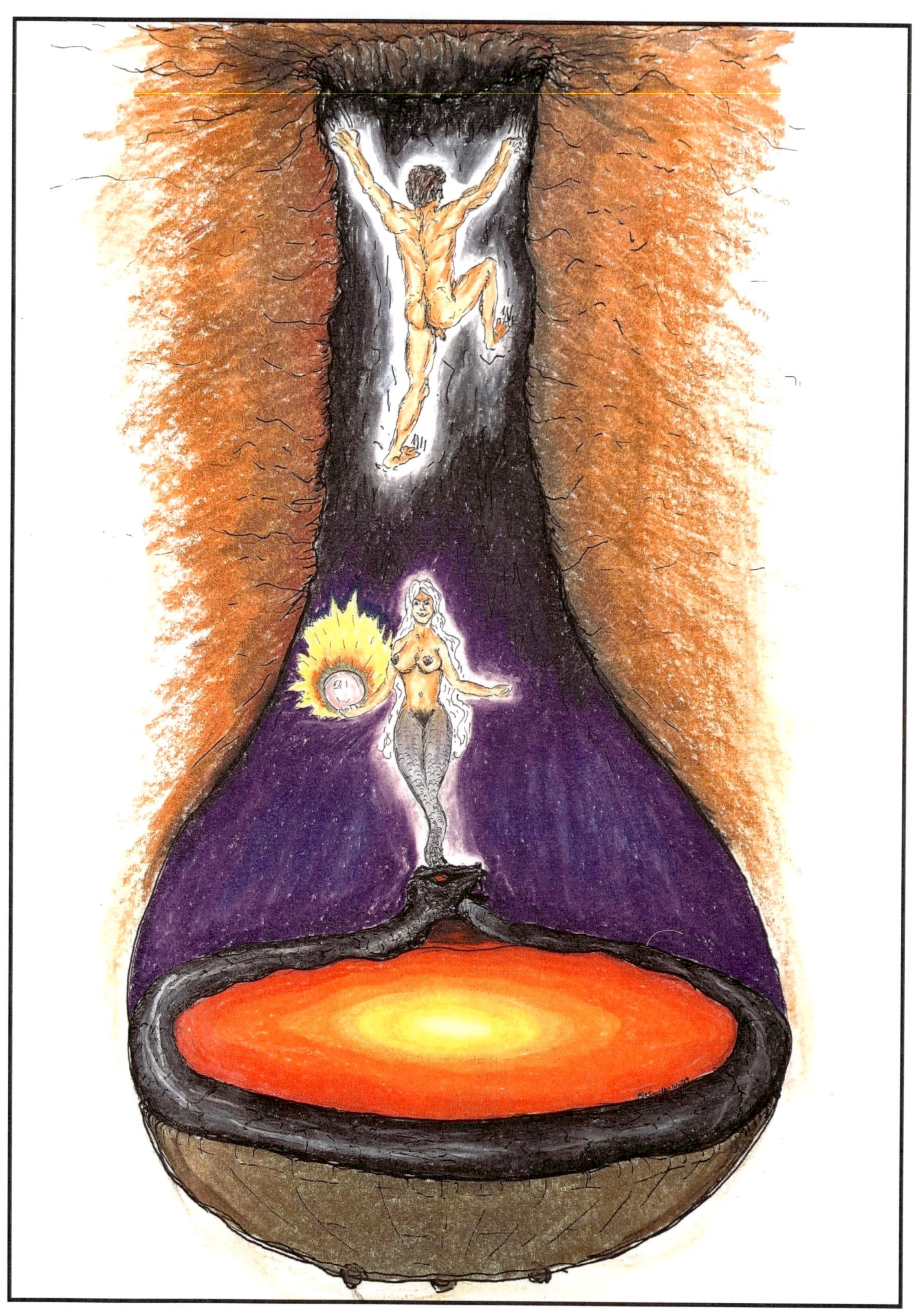

FALLING IN LOVE

This early artwork captures a moment in my life: January 25, 1975, the day I fell in love with my wife. We were together in Vail, Colorado, when suddenly I envisioned a hole opening up beneath me. I fell in but tried to grasp the edges of the hole to prevent my fall. As I slipped downward, I desperately tried to cling to the edges, to resist further plummeting. As the hole widened, I had no choice but to let go, tumbling toward a pool of red-hot lava, which I feared was certain death. When I hit the liquid, it transformed into a warm and loving bath, where my future wife was holding a globe of radiance. Instead of dying, I became embraced by a profound feeling of love for her, and a sense of calm without further fear.

My fall and the accompanying fear reflected my reluctance to enter another committed relationship because of the scars of previous heartbreaks. This experience revealed that I was ready to love again.

More than fifty years later, this vision remains true in my marriage, and I revisit this memory and image often.